THREE JEWS WALKED INTO A SHOPPING CENTER...

A Memoir by
Elizabeth Kraft Taylor

Published & distributed by:
Elizabeth Kraft Taylor

in association with:
IBJ Book Publishing
41 E. Washington St., Suite 200
Indianapolis, IN 46204
www.ibjbp.com

Library of Congress Control Number: 2015939228
ISBN 978-1-939550-20-0
First Edition
Printed in the United States of America

DEDICATION

This book is dedicated to Melvin Simon, Herb Simon, Fred Simon, Gerald Paul, Jerry Gershman, and Jewish men everywhere who give a shiksa a chance.

CONTENTS

PROLOGUE

I am writing this book for three reasons. The first is to honor and remember Melvin Simon. Going to a synagogue to hear his name read aloud once a year is not enough for me. My second reason is to show the honesty and ethical values that were the platform for the incredible success of the Simon organization. Finally, I share my personal story of determination and hope to make the point that we are all born with handicaps and blessings. Our job in life is to figure out which is which.

1

ABOVE THE DRUGSTORE

I was awakened by flashing lights and a policeman saying, "It's a little girl!" He lifted me from my bed, wrapped me in blankets, and carried me down the stairs.

In the parking lot, I saw police cars, a crowd of people and an ambulance. Those flashing red and white lights would become routine in my life, as would being taken to the police station to wait for someone to come and claim me. My mother had just jumped off a third floor porch, her first of many attempts to kill herself.

A big, black steamer trunk sat on our enclosed back porch. She made me get in it when my father was at work and one of her boyfriends was coming over. She was exciting, brilliant, funny, charming, even mesmerizing. She was not beautiful, not even pretty. With small, darting brown eyes and a nose way too big, she had only her super-sized personality and overt sexuality to make her way through the world. She never touched me except to hit, and she liked to beat me with the telephone receiver. My mother was a promiscuous prescription drug addict and child abuser, and eventually addled her brain so badly that she had to be bathed and fed. At age forty-two, she was declared a recluse at the morgue where I identified her body.

When I was four years old, my parents and I lived above a drugstore called Finkleman's on the corner of Madison and Lotus on the far west side of Chicago. Next to the drugstore was a little grocery store—supplier of the mice and cockroaches that shared our apartment upstairs—a children's shoe store and a tavern. We got to our apartment at the rear by way of a gray, peeling wooden jungle of stairs and landings. The stairs rose out of a huge gravel parking lot that accommodated the patrons of all the stores on the block, including drunks from the tavern and a gang of teenage boys. No grass, no trees, just six huge, stinking garbage cans lined the walkway to the stairs.

After my mother's first attempt to kill herself, I came to understand that she didn't want to live, and she particularly didn't want to live with me. Her suicide attempts were varied and numerous so I became hyper vigilant. I couldn't tolerate music or noise in the house because I wanted to be able to hear what my mother was doing at all times.

She was in and out of Loretta Hospital's psychiatric ward where twice she had electroshock therapy. Mother's doctor decided a visit from me might bring her back to reality. Right after my fifth birthday, my father took me to the hospital, and since she had been gone for three weeks, I was excited about seeing her. We were taken behind locked metal doors with small slots for windows.

When they opened the door, I thought the room was empty.

Then I heard something growling in the corner. It was my mother on the floor, bound in a straitjacket, rocking and growling like an animal. Her black hair was matted and wild. The doctor took me to stand in front of her. I was terrified as the noises grew louder. My mother looked at me with horrible, crazy eyes and peed on the floor. I was so close to that little white bound-up animal, I vividly remember the smell and heat of her urine as the brilliant yellow stream pooled on the linoleum floor around her and ran to my black patent leather Mary Janes.

My father lived only for my mother. We all did. She had us convinced that nothing was more important than her and her pills. Every other Friday when my father got paid, I was kept home from school so I could meet him at work and collect his pay. Then I hurried back to Finkleman's to buy her first round of pills for the week. I ran up the stairs with the precious paper bag, the pills bouncing and clicking together all the way.

Through the many hospital stays, mental confinements, miscarriages and arrests, my mother had three more daughters. Laura and Ethel were increasingly abused and neglected as our mother's drug use worsened. Our beautiful baby sister Liane was the most physically impaired, dying of cancer at age thirty-six.

2

MY KIND OF TOWN

I believe I was saved from insanity by a few simple accidents of birth. I was born in Chicago and blessed with an inquisitive, deductive mind and a unique imagination that helped me escape my daily reality.

I followed the shenanigans of our beloved Mayor Richard J. Daley by devouring the *Sun-Times* and, more importantly, the *Chicago Tribune* every day. The government TV channel brought Senators Everett Dirksen and Adlai Stevenson into my life, and they taught me to love words and public speaking. I learned to emulate each one of their speech patterns. I could be a bully like Daley, an orator like Dirksen, and a statesman like Stevenson. I connected with that perfect trifecta of political performers and owe those long dead gentlemen for my ability to present, persuade and sell an idea. They also taught me how to motivate people, friends, acquaintances, a line of random folks at the grocery store, and, on occasion, a pack of small, receptive animals.

I didn't pretend to be a movie star or a ballerina. I pretended to be president of the United States. I assumed an air of authority and walked around the house as though I were about to give the State of the Union Address. Winking at the refrigerator, pointing at the table, pausing to give the dog special attention by shaking his hand, I stepped up to the podium and raised my arms to quiet the applauding crowd. I waited, waited for quiet, then counted a beat of one…two…three. And I began.

> Da mayor had taught me to go to any length to win an argument or a negotiation.

Watching "old man Daley," I became bold. Chicago was the "city that works." We were safe and clean because "da mayor" could see everything—a little like Santa Claus. Daley was proud. He and his city's reputation were one and the same. Daley and Chicago were synonymous and interchangeable. Then one day in September, the garbage men went on strike.

Strikes did NOT happen in Chicago. The city was shocked! We heard the mayor was going to hold a press conference on TV, and suddenly, there he was! In black and white, a short, hefty man with full wet lips, surrounded by much bigger, tough-looking men. Some called them his "goons." He was in front of a podium, papers shaking in his hand. They were probably his speech, but he didn't need papers or a speech because he talked from his heart about how disappointed and embarrassed he was, and then….HE STARTED TO CRY! Da mayor was crying!

He took out a big ole white hankie like all men carried back then and wiped his little eyes and blew his nose. On TV! Then he quickly walked away. There wasn't a sound, only an empty podium on the screen. The announcer said, "Well, I guess that concludes the mayor's press conference."

The next morning, the garbage men went back to work. What else could they do? Stay on strike? Negotiate? No, sir. We were Chicago and da mayor had cried. As young as I was, I knew I had seen something significant. I had seen a man do the unthinkable to get his city back to work. Da mayor had taught me to go to any length to win an argument or a negotiation.

3

MY REFUGE, MY BROADWAY

After the mayor, my second savior was a magnificent store called Madigan's at 4030 Madison Street on the changing west side of Chicago. Both sides of the store had huge display windows enticing customers into the revolving doors that twirled them around to paradise.

The bus to Madigan's cost ten cents and was fifteen stoplights from Finkleman's Drugstore. I sat by the front door, listening to each wheeze and heavy sigh as the bus stopped and started, taking me closer to my glamorous escape. I was only ten years old on my first trip to Madigan's, drawn by their ads in the *Chicago Tribune*. When I realized that I lived on the same Madison Street as Madigan's, I knew I could get there on the bus that, going in the opposite direction, took me to school.

The first floor was cosmetics, jewelry and small accessories, the air perfumed by gorgeous women with big red lips and mascaraed eyes. All the sales ladies got to know me, especially in the jewelry department. When I was old enough to babysit, I bought my first piece of jewelry on layaway, a stunning brooch of turquoise, coral and pearls designed by Kenneth J. Lane. I paid one dollar every Saturday and still wear the brooch today.

A French woman ran the hat department which dominated the second floor. A dozen small dressing tables with mirrors and dainty chairs allowed women to sit and admire themselves in a new chapeau of pink tulle swirled around pink straw; yellow and white daisies on a boater; cloches made of silk violets; turbans of exotic pleated fabrics, and skimmers festooned with roses and lilies of the valley! Mr. John and Oleg Cassini led the parade of labels, each flirty brim suggesting romance. If you wanted a man's attention, you needed to put on a hat.

But it was on the third floor that the real magic happened in the designer department. The elevator doors opened onto plush carpeting, rosy lighting, soft music and beautiful mannequins posed on platforms, wearing evening gowns of periwinkle blue tulle studded with rhinestones or tailored suits with piqué collars and cuffs, a gardenia pinned high on the right shoulder. On Saturdays, live models pranced in pale yellow tea-length dresses, crinolines peeking out with each step, or a black lace cocktail dress glided by, garnished with a dramatic hat. Every woman carried a handbag and wore a hat, high heels and gloves.

Oh, the gloves! Teeny, tiny tucks sewn down the front of starched linen or pale pink rosebuds embroidered on fingertips, the white-on-white brides' gloves, and kid opera gloves with an enormous rhinestone cuff made by Eisenburg clapped around the wrist. I used to stand by the elevator and watch as long as they would let me. Madigan's was my refuge, my Broadway, my motivation, my movies, my secret dreams, and held all my heart's desires. Eventually, I would have to board the bus back home to whatever new horror would be unleashed on us that day.

PAYING TUITION

My sisters and I have memories of abuse and neglect that led to prolonged hospitalizations for all of us. Humiliation, starvation, pain, injury, trauma, loss and betrayal created feelings of shame. I was always covering up what was happening at home, trying to present myself as "just like all the other girls."

We wore uniforms in high school, white blouses and navy blue skirts. It seemed to me that most of the girls had two skirts and several blouses and got new ones each year, but I wore the same clothes all four years. By my senior year, my skirt was in threads. So I got an idea and spent a Saturday covering the inside of my skirt with navy blue duct tape. The skirt was stiff and stuck out in a funny way, but it stayed together for the rest of the year.

It never occurred to me to ask for help because I knew if I were creative and resourceful enough, I could keep passing as a regular person, not as someone with a dozen dirty secrets. I was lonely and lived with shame and longing for someone to love and care for me.

Senior year, the big reward was a trip to a retreat house owned by the nuns. The cost for each student was $300. I had known since my freshman year that I wouldn't be able to afford it, but that year the nuns decided to hold a candy drive. They announced prizes ranging from $25 for the freshman to $100 for the junior selling the most candy. If a senior sold more than $300 worth of candy, she would win a free trip to the retreat house. It was my chance to go, and I knew I could do it!

Then I did the math. We were selling large bars of chocolate for twenty-five cents a bar, and that was 1,200 bars of candy. Holy crap! I decided I would never make it. But I got an idea. With six weeks to sell the candy, I needed to sell fifty bars a week or eight bars a day, more or less. Once I had broken down the task into small increments, I had a strategy.

I sold candy bars on the bus, at the library, at the cleaners and the drugstore, and on the weekends I sold candy door to door. I had no competition because no one else had to win the trip in order to go. If I could just beat the numbers, I could win.

So I did. I sold 1,216 bars of chocolate.

The principal gave daily announcements over the loudspeaker about the competition. On Friday morning of the last week, we would learn the winners. My whole class was aware of what I had done, and my two best friends had given me the money for six bars to help put me over the top. On Friday, I was shaking with excitement. The principal read off the first three prizes and then said she was sorry to announce there was no winner from the senior class.

I felt as if I had been slapped. Was I crazy? Had I dreamed the whole thing? My homeroom was confused, and the girls started whispering as I began to cry. My teacher told me to report to the principal's office. I thought that meant things would get straightened out. But standing in front of the principal, I got the truth. She said that yes, I had sold enough to win the trip and she was sure it had been a difficult task. However, since my parents had not paid my tuition, the nuns had decided the prize money should go toward my tuition and not the trip.

Too ashamed to tell the truth, I told my classmates I must have miscounted.

5

GETTING PAID FOR IT

My fate was sealed one day when I was looking through the *Chicago Tribune* want ads. Madigan's was seeking a person to work in its display department. I didn't know anything about display, but I wanted to work at Madigan's so badly, I would have done anything to get a job there.

I interviewed and was hired to work with a group of three other display women. We designed and merchandised new store windows every two weeks, dressing mannequins in every window and throughout the store. Our displays were designed to teach customers how to wear the latest fashions, how to combine the newest colors, and how to dip their new hats over one eye.

Because of the physical nature of our work, we were allowed to wear slacks and flat shoes while all other female employees were required to wear skirts or dresses, nylon stockings and high heels.

Display props were stored a half block away in a warehouse stocked with plastic flowers, Roman columns, arbors, furniture, painted screens, Santa Claus thrones, mannequins and lots of other stuff. Everything had been spray-painted a dozen times to make it look fresh and new. We carted and dragged our paraphernalia down the block, sometimes wearing items on our heads that we couldn't carry in our arms. One day, Mr. Madigan saw me walking down Madison Street with boobs on my head. He politely asked me to stop transporting female bust forms in that particular manner.

Retailers took themselves seriously in those days and followed the rule book for merchandise display to the letter. No lingerie or delicates could be shown on a mannequin. Only straight pins with pearl heads could be used to attach merchandise to forms. Men and women mannequins shown together wore wedding rings, as did female mannequins with children. Mannequins weren't allowed to touch each other. These rules restricted our creative freedom, but the world was changing and soon retail would also evolve.

In order to teach myself everything possible and learn quickly, I read every fashion and retail magazine available. *Women's Wear Daily, Vogue, Bazaar* and *Chain Store Age* were my textbooks. I was interested in business more than the art of display, so I watched the sales figures and year-to-date sales comparisons. I had found my passion in retail, and I was getting paid for it!

THE DAY AFTER
THE NIGHT BEFORE

It was Friday and my day to teach art at St. Patrick's Academy, a grammar school run by the Sisters of Mercy at the corner of Oakley Avenue and Washington Boulevard.

Only 120 students, most of them from the wealthiest Catholic families in Chicago, attended the school. Many lived in the ritzy suburbs of River Forest and Oak Brook and were picked up by a school bus. Other students arrived in black cars or limousines. Twice a month, Madigan's allowed me the day off to conduct art classes at St. Patrick's.

I rode the bus to school that morning with the kids. As the double doors opened, the children started clapping and screaming, "Good morning, Miss Kraft!" Six or seven little ones sat on the bench seat behind the driver, waiting to pounce on me. They piled on, their tiny hands swarming to catch my hand or dress.

That day, April 5, 1968, after class started, I thought I heard gun shots, then shouting, sirens and more sirens. Martin Luther King, Jr. had been assassinated in Memphis the night before, and we were in the heart of Chicago's ghetto. Noise outside the building was growing louder and closer, then I smelled smoke. A nun came into my classroom and whispered that we were in the middle of a riot.

Buildings all around us had been set on fire, and roving gangs were looting and destroying everything in their path. Desperate parents were calling the school or trying to drive through the police lines, but an area of several miles had turned into a war zone and was closed off to incoming traffic. Our calls to the police went unanswered.

The nuns and I began quickly moving students into the gymnasium, bringing together brothers, sisters and cousins. The gym had no windows, and the noises from outside were terrifying. Rocks thudded against the building, hurled bottles shattered on the pavement, and voices chanted and screamed. Smoke was filling the hallways. The old bus driver, ten dozen kids, a handful of nuns and I sat on the floor trying to give every child a hand to hold. The nuns started praying the rosary as children sat shaking, crying, and some even wetting their pants.

We had to take a chance and move the kids out of the school because the smoke was so dense, it was getting hard to breathe. Since the school bus was parked in a walled courtyard just outside the gym door, we could open the school doors and create a safe passageway for the kids. If the children crawled onto the bus, we might be able to drive out of the area, looking like an empty school bus. There was no other viable option.

The nuns called the parents and directed them to meet us in Oak Park while I explained to the children how we were going to get home. To look like an empty school bus, we had to lie down together all the way home. With no complaints, everybody squeezed onto the school bus. The little ones cried quietly until some got hiccups. That tiny sound was heartbreaking.

The bus rolled through streets where people were being dragged from their cars and beaten. Our vehicle was hit by rocks and bricks but continued to inch along. After about forty-five minutes, the noise outside seemed to have calmed down, so I raised my head to peek out. On the corner, a small crowd of people stood waiting for a city bus. Black and white people were standing together, bleeding, their clothes torn, their faces swollen and scratched. They had come out of a factory, beaten each other up, and then waited together for public transportation to take them home. That strange, confusing scene still sticks in my brain.

Finally, Oak Park came into view. We were safe. As parents grabbed their children, the eastern sky behind us blackened with smoke that choked the proud city of Chicago. That night, Mayor Daley ordered the police to "shoot to kill arsonists and shoot to maim looters." In all, nine people were killed, more than a thousand left homeless, and about twenty-five hundred people were arrested.

By the following Tuesday, public transportation had been reinstated, and I returned to work under the eyes of the National Guard driving tanks up and down Madison Street. After getting off the bus, everyone had to show identification and proof of employment in the area. There was no business, no traffic, and for a long time to come, little hope or trust for the citizens of Chicago.

Four months later in August, the Democrats showed up for their national convention. Didn't anyone think a political convention might have gone better in Peoria? That summer, Robert F.

Kennedy had been assassinated just two months after Martin Luther King Jr. was murdered. In every large city in America, anti-Vietnam War protests were being organized. Mayor Daley had planned to showcase his city's achievements to the Democrats and the news media. Instead, the convention became notorious for a bloody clash between 10,000 demonstrators and 23,000 police officers and National Guardsmen.

"Gestapo tactics on the streets of Chicago!" cried the media. Under Daley's order, the beatings of demonstrators and the media began, then came the tear gas and paddy wagons. As remarkable as it would still be today, public opinion polls showed the majority of Americans supported the mayor's tactics, and he won the next election by a landslide.

On the day of his death, December 20, 1976, Mayor Daley attended a Christmas breakfast with his staff and went on to a dedication ceremony for a new gymnasium. He was asked to shoot the first basket and sank the ball on his first try. But by early afternoon, he was dead of a heart attack. Daley died as he had lived, serving Chicago, and never knowing what he had done for a little girl on his city's far west side.

7

SMOKE INHALATION

On September 3, 1969, my sisters left for their first day back at school, and I went to work at Madigan's. Three hours later a neighbor called and told me our apartment was on fire.

My sisters were safe in school, but our mother, who was a recluse by that time, was at home. One of my coworkers drove me home, and as we neared our apartment, I jumped from the car and ran past the fire engines and police cars into the building and up two flights of stairs.

My mother's bedroom door was closed, so I shoved it open. Everything was black. Flat, flat black. The fire had turned everything to cinders except a silhouette of my mother's body where she had fallen on the mustard-colored hardwood floor. Her body had been removed, leaving spongy charred flesh stuck to the floor, the smell of it overwhelming. I went into the closet, shut the door and hid. A fireman found me and led me downstairs.

When my father arrived, the police told us to go to the emergency room. As we rode to the hospital, he kept asking if I thought Mother was still alive. I couldn't tell him I had just been standing in her blackened flesh. All I knew was that the nightmare was over, and that by the grace of God and the school calendar year, my sisters were still alive. I was flooded with gratitude and relief. The hospital confirmed that our mother had perished in the fire and her body had been taken to the Cook County Morgue.

My three sisters were waiting for me at a neighbor's house. When I explained our mother had died in the fire, they were silent and wide-eyed. I had to tell my baby sister Liane that her bird had also perished. She screamed and cried out, "But I loved my bird!" My other sisters consoled her and talked about how great her bird had been. They said it had loved her back. No one mentioned our mother.

That night, sitting in what was left of our apartment and trying to ignore the smell, we finally talked about our mother. We all felt a sense of relief that she was gone and had not taken any of us with her. We made lists of all the ways she couldn't hurt or embarrass us any more. The evening developed into a little celebration with my sisters singing, "Ding, dong the witch is dead." Our father had taken refuge at the corner tavern.

After the fire, my work life went into overdrive. On Sundays I cooked breakfast and lunch for the Sisters of Mercy at their convent to help pay my sisters' tuition. Eight to five, Monday through Friday, I worked at Madigan's. In the summer my night job began at ten p.m. at Sportsman's Race Track, cleaning the stands after the horse races.

Every night I crawled through the stands on my hands and knees with a shopping bag over each arm. The garbage I picked up with my right hand went into the shopping bag over my left arm, and the garbage that I picked up with my left hand went into the shopping bag over my right arm. Right to left, left to right. Cigarette butts, ticket stubs, gum, beer cans, plastic cups...right to left, left to right.

8

MINISKIRTS AND
AN EGG TIMER

Mini-skirts, bouffant hairdos, boots and white lipstick defined the first look of the early seventies.

British designers like Mary Quant and teenage fashion model Twiggy with her ultra-thin, androgynous demeanor created a cult following that led to a whole new retail niche, the junior department. The seventies was boom time for trendy stores that catered to this market. Casual Corner, The Limited and Paul Harris stores battled for the best space in every mall and for every nickel this new customer could spend.

Mr. Madigan fully embraced this emerging demographic and focused on clothing for juniors at prices that teenagers could afford. He realized he needed help in creating a more youthful and bold image for his stores now spread out in the western suburbs of Chicago. His most successful store was located in a mall owned by Melvin Simon & Associates, North Riverside Park. I later learned that Madigan's was the most successful store in all of the Simon malls.

Because of my interest in the business side of retail and because I drove everyone crazy with my "good ideas," I had been transferred into the advertising department. To get the junior campaign started, a visual merchandising position was created, and Tim Berglund came on board. He was an articulate, trailblazing genius who immediately won Mr. Madigan's confidence.

Tim knew our advertising needed dramatic change, and he liked my ideas, energy and enthusiasm for retail. He convinced Mr. Madigan to promote me to director of advertising. Since I didn't have a college education, I never thought I would be more than a clerk, and without typing skills, I couldn't even qualify as a secretary. And yet suddenly, I was director of advertising in the store of my childhood dreams! Then the creation of Madigan's new image began. We hired the best talent from the best stores in the city and a whole cast of characters from other retailers around the country.

Our newspaper ads and store windows became famous, with crowds gathering every time we opened new displays. We floated mannequins in the air, wearing skimpy lingerie and large feathered angel wings, which Victoria's Secret does today. One Halloween, we contrived female mannequins with three breasts and four arms. At our Woodfield Mall grand opening, we produced a short version of the Broadway smash *Pippin*, using the escalators to stage a moving fashion show.

Tim won Display Man of the Year for three years in a row, a national competition among stores such as Bloomingdale's and Marshall Field's. Madigan's sales went through the roof, with every clothing department benefiting from the increased traffic brought in by our focus on the junior customer.

My time with Joe Madigan and Tim Berglund sharpened my presentation skills—Tim, because he was so well-spoken and precise, and Mr. Madigan because he kept an egg timer on his desk. Each time I stepped into his office to make a presentation, he turned over the egg timer. As I spoke, I kept one eye on his face and the other on the running sands that would bring our meeting to a close. Those two men taught me to use language and time effectively.

Then Mr. Madigan decided to update the store in North Riverside Park. The excitement about that grand opening centered on the rumor that the

> Since I didn't have a college education, I never thought I would be more than a clerk ... suddenly, I was director of advertising in the store of my childhood dreams!

Simon brothers were coming to our party. I was out of my mind with curiosity about the Simons because on two previous visits, Mr. Madigan had told me to stay in my office until they left the building. How incredibly tantalizing! What kind of magnetism, what kind of power did these men possess that compelled Mr. Madigan to quarantine me in my office?

At the party I stood with Mr. Madigan as those three magnificent Jews walked into the shopping center. The air seemed electrified, and a little voice in my head said, "I belong with those guys." I couldn't have guessed they would become my Three Wise Men, bringing me gifts of opportunity, self-worth and trust.

When I saw Fred Simon at the buffet table, I walked right up and started talking. We discussed Madigan's, the mall we were in, other malls with a Madigan's, malls the Simons owned, and retail stores in general from Macy's to Tiffany's. Most likely as a ploy to get away from me, Fred said that I should come and work for Simon in Indianapolis.

Fate knew that I was not ready for them, and they were certainly not ready for me! I would have to wait ten more years, so the idea shimmered in my brain for the next decade.

After a few years, I started thinking about leaving Madigan's to see if I could be successful with people who hadn't helped me grow up. A group of men's stores called Four Squires located in the far western suburbs advertised an opening. The job came with a car, and even though I didn't know how to drive, I applied. I wanted a car and figured this would force me to learn to drive. A friend took me to the interview thirty-six miles away.

A week later I was hired, gave Madigan's my two weeks notice, and started driving lessons every evening. I was thirty years old and had ridden the bus everywhere I ever needed to go. My new bosses were shocked that my first day of work was also the first day I had ever driven by myself anywhere. For Christmas, they gave me a motorcycle helmet to wear in my car because I had trouble turning corners at an appropriate speed.

My business education continued in this job. I learned about free-standing stores in small downtowns like Elgin, Wheaton and Rockford. I also learned about a range of topics from antiques and auctions to barbecuing. All the partners in Four Squires were family men who mentored me in financial matters. One day, Harold Gadae took me aside and told me it was time for me to buy a house. I had no idea how much a house cost or that I'd saved enough money to buy one. I was surprised to learn I could afford a down payment.

My sisters and I moved into a house on Grove Avenue in Oak Park. Our lives there were adventuresome and hilarious because we continued to live as adolescents. Like Peter Pan, we did not want to grow up. I didn't know how to do anything but work, which isolated me from experiences my girlfriends were having. All around me, young women were getting engaged and married. I couldn't understand it. The whole idea of being that close to someone was unthinkable. Intimacy and sex? Not on my radar. I lived in a female world safe from emotional entanglements.

Pulling into the Four Squires parking lot on a sweltering August day in 1977, a news bulletin stopped me from turning off the radio. Elvis Presley was dead in Memphis at the age of forty-two. The same age my mother had died. I walked into my office, picked up the phone, and starting calling stores in downtown Chicago to see who was hiring. Suddenly, life seemed very short, and I wanted a bigger challenge.

THAT GREAT STREET

State Street in downtown
Chicago was one of the retail
nirvanas of the world! After
learning as much about retail
and advertising as I could at
Madigan's and Four Squires,
I was hired as creative director
at Charles A. Stevens, a large
group of women's fashion stores.

I worked in the State Street store in downtown Chicago, and my
job was creating and overseeing production of all newspaper ads,
catalogs and television commercials.

Working with talented fashion photographers, models and
clothing designers was exciting and glamorous! Yet even in such
a creative environment, a conventional approach to advertising
was expected by management. To evaluate the competition and

feed my brain, I spent lunch hours trolling other stores, especially at Water Tower Place, a vertical mall being built and leased on Michigan Boulevard. Its two-story escalator rose through the middle of the atrium, and each week I rode it to visit the new specialty stores opening every day.

One day, about to step on the up escalator, I glanced at the traffic coming down and gasped! I swear I heard music as the most handsome, best-dressed gentleman I ever saw rode the stairs toward me. And smiled.

A voice in my head said, "I'm going to marry that guy."

I wasn't surprised to get a glimpse of my future because I'd heard that voice before, telling me what was to come.

Every day, wearing my best outfits, I ran over to Water Tower Place and rode up and down the escalator, hoping to see him once more.

Nothing. The music was silent, the prince had vanished. I wouldn't see him again for thirty years. After I had moved to Indianapolis and he'd returned to his hometown, Zionsville, Indiana, we married on September 7, 2011.

At work, I began to realize my creativity was not highly valued when management blocked one of my best ideas. The day the Chicago Transit Authority (CTA) went on strike and the El shut down, I put together an ad that read, "Here's a Token of Our Affection," with a photograph of a subway token. The ad promised a free token to ride the CTA after the strike for anyone who shopped at our store during the strike.

Management refused to run my ad because "it didn't sell merchandise." I told them the ad would create goodwill and be the talk of the city. Nope. Well, that made me furious, so I marched my ad across the street to Marshall Field's who ran it the next day. Management at Charles A. Stevens didn't get it. They thought the ad was a coincidence.

Later, when the director of advertising resigned, management told me I could not be promoted because I didn't have a college degree. Instead, a store manager with a degree in home economics became director of advertising.

I knew I needed to find a different job for many reasons and felt confident I was ready to move in a more ambitious direction. Not to mention, my sisters and I were at risk of ending up little old maids living together forever.

It was time to shake things up. And then...

Wanted: Creative Director
Wild, Undisciplined, Sometimes Rebellious, Raw Talent Seeks Leadership

Melvin Simon & Associates, the nation's second largest shopping center developer, has an award-winning creative staff of 10 growing to 13. Due to present economics, this staff needs an iron fist in a velvet glove to lead them, kicking and screaming, into the cold, cruel world of retail advertising. They know soft-sell retail, but no one has hooked them on the hard stuff. As Creative Director, you would be responsible for enlightening, educating, guiding, leading, and, now and then, roughing up this motley crew. A minimum of four years experience as a Creative Director or Associate Creative Director in retail oriented accounts is required. You'll be paid competitively...and you'll earn every dime of it. You'll get medical, dental and life insurance, and you get to live in Indianapolis.

Send resume and salary requirements to:

Tom Hovanec

P.O. Box 7033
Indianapolis, Indiana 46207
An equal opportunity employer.

35

10

TWO INTERVIEWS

From the tone of the employment ad for creative director, I knew Simon & Associates was the right workplace for me. I sent in my resume.

A few weeks later, a call came from the Simon personnel department, requesting that I meet with Tom Hovanac for breakfast at a hotel in downtown Chicago.

"Absolutely, yes," I said.

Tom and I started our interview at eight and were still going strong at eleven-thirty. I agreed to fly to Indianapolis the following week for interviews with three Simon executives.

My last meeting was with Herb Simon. We got into a discussion about common area maintenance charges against retailers, and gradually the interview turned into a full-fledged argument. Voices were raised.

"You don't know anything about shopping centers!" Herb said, standing up.

Knowing the interview was over, and I would never see Herb Simon again as long as I lived, I shouted, "That's okay because you don't know anything about retail!"

I was supposed to go back to the personnel department, but I was so furious, I got a cab to the airport, and there I sat, filled with regret, waiting for my flight.

Then I got a second chance. Lynn Wilson in Simon's marketing department invited me to Simon's national convention for their mall managers and marketing directors. She wanted me to speak about a retailer's perspective on shopping centers. My invitation was for one day, but I stayed four. I began to see I could make a difference at Simon. My retail background and training would bring a new voice to the table.

After the convention, I began to do consulting with retailers who were unhappy in one Simon mall or another, to help them with their retail problems. Eventually I had a second interview at the Simon home office, behaved professionally, and got the creative director job.

Leaving my sisters behind was difficult, but I needed to pursue my dreams. After I left, they began to grow into young women who married, had children, and lived their own lives, too.

11

MY FIRST FORAY

After I was hired as creative director at Simon, my first assignment was to figure out a marketing plan for a mixed use building on the corner of Washington and Meridian Streets in Indianapolis.

I named it Two West Washington and began preparing my first presentation for the Simon brothers. I was thirty-two years old and entering a male-dominated industry.

The day of my presentation, I walked into a small room that was like a circus. The energy was electric, phones ringing

Fred Simon took the cigar out of his mouth and started laughing. "You're going to do all right here, girlie."

everywhere. Cigars, back slapping, jokes—it was the locker room after a win. I'd never encountered such an atmosphere in the workplace before. My presentation was interrupted five or six times. No one was listening to me because they were all performing for each other. This wasn't a workplace! It was Theatre of the Absurd.

When one of the guys started drawing on my ads, saying I should change this and that, I joined the band of thespians. Taking the artwork out of his hand, I looked him in the eye, crumpled up the ad, and threw it over my shoulder.

"I am going to do the marketing here," I said. "Or you're going to do the marketing here. But both of us are not going to do the marketing here."

Silence.

Stillness.

Fred Simon took the cigar out of his mouth and started laughing. "You're going to do all right here, girlie."

I packed up my presentation and left, getting to the parking lot before I started shaking. Suddenly, I realized that not everything I had learned at Madigan's, Four Squires, and Charles A. Stevens was going to transfer to my job at Simon. No more egg timers or afternoon teas, and the prissy navy dress with the white collar and cuffs had to be burned. That day, I began the journey to becoming the person I had always wanted to be—bold, strong, outspoken and uninhibited. And when that didn't scare anyone, I became comfortable with myself for the first time. I lost fifty pounds and became a beautiful young woman. Simon was the perfect environment for me. I flourished and bloomed. Those were my "glory days," and I loved every minute of the high-stakes game we played for the next dozen years.

12

4057 N. MERIDIAN

The money I made selling my house in Oak Park went much farther in Indianapolis.

So I was able to buy a home in a gorgeous old residential neighborhood called Meridian-Kessler. If you want everyone to know your business, live on Meridian Street in Indianapolis, the city's main north-south corridor lined with old mansions.

I moved in during October of 1980 and for Halloween put a white ceramic ghost in my front window. When he was plugged in at night, his eyes lit up. Later, Herb Simon told me that people assumed I was very religious because they thought my Halloween ghost was a statue of the Virgin Mary.

13

NICE TO MEET YOU, TOO!

Eleven months into my job at Simon, I was promoted to marketing director and took over the special events department.

This gave me responsibility for producing mall grand openings and corporate events. My first grand opening was scheduled for August of 1981 in a Navy town near the Atlantic Ocean, Lynn Haven Mall at Virginia Beach, Virginia. We invited, as our celebrities, the Benny Goodman Orchestra and Victoria Principal, a star in the number one television show, *Dallas*.

At the time, Victoria was dating a man from the wildly popular Bee Gees trio. In lieu of money for her appearance, she requested that a white baby grand piano be delivered to her boyfriend. Not as simple as it sounds, but she was so popular, we would have carried the piano on our backs, if necessary, to get her to come to the grand opening.

After the public opening of the mall, we hosted a dinner party that evening for our partners and associates. As dessert was served, the fireworks show began as if it were rising from the ocean. The fireworks dazzled the sky and reflected in the water. For the finale, the Lynn Haven Mall logo in pale blue brilliance shot up, hung in the sky, and dissolved into the night.

Jubilant, Melvin dispensed toasts and praises from the head table, paying tribute to everyone involved in putting the mall together. After a long list of compliments and congratulations, he said, "Where is this Eliz Kraft I've heard so much about?"

I didn't know what to do until the men at my table told me to stand up. As I rose, standing alone in the room full of strangers, Melvin said, "I've heard all about you. I heard you've been here for days, and I heard all you do is lay on the beach all day and screw somebody all night."

I didn't have to think. "Well, Mr. Simon, which one of those two things is bothering you the most?" I shot back.

After a moment, Melvin threw back his head and roared with laughter. We were worthy opponents.

14

A FAST RIDE

My Meridian Street house was a yellow brick traditional home, much too large for me, but it reminded me of Chicago and Oak Park in particular.

Since the house sat a hundred feet back from the street, garbage was collected at the curb. Like many of my neighbors, I filled my car with garbage bags on trash day and drove them to the end of the driveway. This was an effective plan until one summer morning, I headed out to the airport and forgot to unload the garbage.

The minute I turned left out of my driveway onto Meridian, I remembered the trash. The morning rush hour made it impossible to turn back, so I decided to dump the bags at the airport. No problem. However, when I got to the airport, there were no large garbage cans in the parking lot. I had a plane to catch, so I locked my car, figuring the garbage would have to cook in the blazing sun for a couple of days until I got home. There was nothing else I could do.

On my return trip, I changed planes in Chicago. The flight to Indianapolis almost always had other Simon employees on board, and that day a Simon vice president was waiting at the gate in O'Hare when I checked in. He was one of those well-groomed, beautifully tailored men who never, ever looked as if he had been dragged backwards through a zoning meeting or had seen six shopping centers in two days. I'd worked with Barry Lindsey on my first project, Two West Washington, as he was in charge of downtown Indianapolis. Before boarding, we made colleague small talk, then he sat in first class and I went back to economy.

Later at baggage pickup, he said he'd left Indianapolis on a corporate jet and his car was at Combs Gates, a private hanger at the airport. Could I give him a lift? Of course, no problem. I didn't remember the garbage until we were on the parking lot shuttle bus. Oh, SHIT!

To cause a distraction and obstruct the inevitable, I started looking around to see if there were any way I could injure myself. Nothing. Maybe I could fall off the bus? In desperation, I decided to pretend I couldn't find my car. To make this deception work, I had to pass the stop where I'd left my car and get off at the next. With Barry trailing, I wandered up and down the rows of vehicles, carrying my suitcases, briefcase and handbag, sweating and stopping to adjust the load. Barry followed along, crisp and composed with his single small leather grip. I mumbled something about not seeing my car.

"It should be in this section, but…maybe…no, it's got to be…."

Finally, I faced Barry and said my car must have been stolen. I should call the police, and he should grab a cab, I said. "Really, just go!"

Barry started walking to the bus pickup and suddenly called out, "Eliz, here it is! Everything's all right!"

I said that wasn't my car.

"Yes, it is. Look!"

"No, no. Oh… maybe it is."

I pressed down on my keyring fob to unlock my door first. A heat wave rushed out, carrying a smell. A big smell. A noxious, stinking smell. Barry was hit by it a moment later. His head rocked back, his eyes bulged. We both slipped into the car, neither of us saying a word. I could see him holding his breath, and my eyes were tearing from the heat and stench.

I drove as fast as I could to Combs Gates where he jumped out and bent over, gasping for air. He never thanked me for the ride.

15

WHAT A PUTZ!

My partner in crime for most of the shenanigans I pulled off on a weekly basis was a giant of a man named Rodney Putz, a most unusual name. Unbelievably, his first wife was named Royal.

Rodney was not any ordinary executive. He had a huge physical presence and a mind that kept dozens of projects going simultaneously. The fact that we both blazed with energy and had a sense of humor about ourselves made us allies. We were a perfect team for opening all those malls.

Rodney and I always set up a war room in the middle of the mall where we held meetings, ate meals, and left notes to communicate with each other. From that room we commanded separate armies. His was management, mine was marketing. Our first day at any mall with workmen still on site, Rodney and I swore construction would never get finished in time. Construction always looked about three weeks behind, some permit had not yet been granted, and sawdust and debris were everywhere. And then the emergencies would begin––bomb threats, leaking pipes, protestors in the parking lot.

Rodney always rented some kind of electric conveyance and roared around the mall with both enormous fists full of local food. If we were in Texas, it was ribs. On the east coast, it was lobster rolls. He knew great family-owned restaurants in every city with a Simon mall. Evenings, we often gathered our teams and drove over bumpy dirt roads or took taxis into Mexico to slip down alleyways to unmarked doors for a meal.

Two or three days before an opening, dozens of home office personnel swarmed into the new location, and we all did whatever it took to get the mall ready, even if it meant cleaning. Pushing a million square feet of property into existence was not for the fastidious.

Looking like the circus had just arrived, we all stayed in the same hotel and wore old clothes we could toss in the trash on our way out of town. Showing up in the same clothes two days in a row did not mean you were doing the walk of shame, but rather that you had fallen asleep in your clothes and were too tired to do anything but get back to the mall the next morning.

A mall opening was an intense experience, sort of out-of-body, and strange things happened. At Lynn Haven, I ran from one end of the mall to the other with my foot bothering me. I didn't take time to remove my shoe but only to shake my foot and then move on. All day, walk, walk, shake, walk, walk. Late that night when I took off my gym shoes, I found a small hair curler inside, the metal kind with bristles.

16

TEN THOUSAND DOLLARS

My hotel room looked like the set for a porn movie. Mirrors had been installed on the ceiling above the large round bed and also on the walls of the Jacuzzi.

This was my first trip to Las Vegas. I left the room and walked around the hotel, the MGM Grand, trying to accustom my eyes to the red and gold environment. My plan was to meet other Simon executives at the front door and go across the street to Caesar's Palace for dinner.

After the group had gathered, I pushed through the revolving doors and went out to cross the street. Suddenly a strong arm pulled me back. It was Rodney Putz.

"Where do you think you're going? The cars aren't here yet."

"Cars? I thought we were just going across the street."

"We are, but you just can't walk across the street in Las Vegas! How would that look? We have to wait for the limos," he said. "And by the way, keep a straight face when you meet Melvin's driver."

"Why? Is something wrong with him?"

"Nothing, other than his name is Oral." Rodney grinned.

I waited as instructed, wondering what other peculiar customs were practiced in Vegas. When we got to Caesar's, by driving around the block, we were greeted like family and taken to a private room for dinner. Was this custom number two? Did we not eat in public in Vegas?

The walls of our dining room were pale cream silk, waterfall chandeliers hung from carvings in the ceilings, and floral still lifes graced the walls. Our dining table was laden with fresh flowers and some of the most beautiful china and gold flatware I had ever seen. I was so excited, I must have seemed naive. My colleagues' attitude appeared to be, "Let's show the kid the ropes."

"The ropes" in Las Vegas separated the men from the boys, or the plain rich from the Super Rich. The ropes were thick red velvet cords that hung from stanchions and were heavily guarded because they secured the entry to the high rollers private gambling rooms. There must have been a password or secret signal because the ropes dropped immediately as we approached. Every time.

Once inside the high stakes magic kingdom, the air seemed rarified and the sights astonishing. One night I saw a Middle Eastern gentleman dressed in a white silk robe at a roulette wheel. He stood, placing tall stacks of orange chips while a woman behind him rubbed his buttocks.

I also saw Melvin at a black jack table where participation required a minimum of $10,000 a throw. I lingered for a while, watching him play.

"Melvin," I finally said, "you just lost more than you pay me in a year."

"Eliz," he answered, "you've got to learn to be a better negotiator."

17

BOYS CLUB

Back in the day, real estate development was strictly a man's world, and some of my colleagues were unprepared to share their domain with a woman.

When I was promoted to director of marketing, I moved into my former boss's office. His desk faced the door, so upon entering, the first thing anyone saw was my head peeking up from behind an enormous desk. I was sitting on three Indianapolis phone books.

After requesting new furniture more suited to my height, I went with Rodney to our purchasing agent, Bob, to plan a new office. Months went by. I flew out of town dozens of times, expecting after each trip to come home to new office furniture. Nothing ever arrived, not a chair, a desk or even a plant. Finally, I called Rodney and asked him to check on my furniture.

Rodney had some very telling habits. When he was happy or excited, he rubbed his hands together as though washing them.

When he was upset, he rubbed his forehead and cheeks. I knew something was wrong when Rodney appeared at my office door, furiously rubbing his face.

"Bob didn't order your furniture," he said. Rub, rub.

"What?" I couldn't believe it. "Why?"

> While getting off a jet, I tripped in a pothole and fell on the tarmac. "Someone pick up the broad!" one of the boys shouted.

Rub, rub. "He didn't think you would last long, so he didn't order any furniture."

It wasn't easy being a woman living in Boys Town. Once while getting off a jet with a bunch of mall managers and construction guys, I tripped in a pothole and fell on the tarmac, ripping my hands and knees, shredding my nylons, and tearing my suit. The contents of my purse and briefcase flew everywhere.

"Someone pick up the broad!" one of the boys shouted back to our pilots.

They didn't even slow down but left for the meeting without me while I got medical attention in the airport office.

18

IT'S A SECRET

A disembodied voice tense with urgency came over my intercom. "Melvin wants to see you RIGHT NOW!"

Melvin's door was shut. At Simon, doors were never closed, so I didn't know what to think. I knocked and the door opened a crack. An arm reached out, pulled me inside, and slammed the door behind me. Melvin stood there with five or six other men.

I looked up to read his face. Calm, untroubled, happy. I relaxed and took a breath. "What can I do?" I asked.

"This is a secret you can't tell anyone," he said.

"All right."

"We just bought the Pacers!"

"Oh."

"Do you want to market them? It's another big job, but if you want it, it's yours. Take the weekend and think about it."

"Okay."

"Let me know on Monday."

"Yes, of course." I inched toward the door.

Once in the hall, I ran to my office and called in Teri Moore and Victor Ruthig. Teri was our chief copywriter, and Vic ran our special events department.

"What are the Pacers?" I asked.

"They're Indiana's NBA basketball team, the only pro team in the state," Vic said.

Teri added, "They're under-marketed, have no money and very little attendance at their games. They're at the bottom of the league."

"In a state that's crazy for basketball!" Vic yelled.

> "We just bought the Pacers!" "What are the Pacers?"

"Great, thanks," I said. I started back to Melvin's office, thinking this was an unbelievable opportunity.

Then, it hit me. Melvin and Herb had just purchased an NBA franchise! How many people got to do that in a lifetime? And how many people would turn around and offer the opportunity to market such a high profile new enterprise to a staff member with no sports experience? It was a strong statement of their belief in me and also of their way of running their company. If Melvin and Herb thought they could do something, they wanted us all to do it together. Their management style was changing the way I viewed the world and myself.

"First of all, let me offer you my congratulations," I told Melvin. "This must seem like a dream come true. Mazel tov, Mr. Simon. And secondly, I would be thrilled to be a part of this new venture."

"Eliz, really think about it," he said. "There are people in place over there who will be sensitive about us taking over. There's a lot of work to do. I want the city to be proud of the Pacers," Melvin said.

"You mean you want the city to have Pacer Pride?"

Melvin beamed.

19

PACER PRIDE

We had our tagline, Pacer Pride, so it was easy to prepare for the press conference announcing the Simons' acquisition of the Pacers.

All we needed was a TV commercial, a radio jingle, bumper stickers, a billboard, T-shirts, a gazillion blue and gold balloons, and some promotional pins. And we had two days to get it all accomplished.

I knew nothing about basketball but figured the marketing strategies we used in the malls would also work for pro ball. My department had learned to combine creativity, unbounded energy and willingness to work hard behind the scenes into a recognizable way of doing business. We would bring to the Pacers what had become known as "Simon style."

The atmosphere at the announcement was electric. "We have placed great faith in the Hoosier sense of pride, and we pledge to you a year of excitement, entertainment and competition worthy of Indiana's rich basketball tradition," Herb Simon said to the spirited crowd.

We wanted to keep building the city's enthusiasm throughout the season ticket campaign. My event staff and the Pacer staff met with Melvin and Herb to give them our vision for opening night of the NBA season.

"It's a start-over for the city. It's a rebirth for the team. It's champagne and celebration!" I said with passion. "We can make it look like a Hollywood opening. We want it to be black tie!"

The brothers looked at each other, and one of them rolled his eyes. But as I explained the national and local publicity we could garner, and promised to sell out Market Square Arena, I could see them coming around. Randy Foxworthy, our general counsel, told the brothers not to count on selling out the arena.

"Don't listen to Eliz. It will never happen," he insisted.

Randy made his prediction based on previous Pacer game attendance of not more than 3,000 people in an arena seating 16,530 basketball fans. My prediction came from my belief in the power of the right message to the public at the right time. I also had my usual confidence and spunk.

Once Melvin and Herb had agreed to don their tuxes, we ran with the idea of a huge black tie event. Ray Compton from the Pacer staff had the brainstorm to print commemorative T-shirts like the front of a tuxedo. We could always go forward fast, gathering momentum with each passing day once the brothers had committed to an idea because they did not renege or second guess us. Their trust in us, and in all of their employees, was what encouraged our success and theirs.

The evening started with a VIP champagne cocktail reception at the convention center. We invited local politicians, our business associates, and those who had purchased season tickets. They all showed up in black tie. We paraded from the convention center to Market Square Arena with Melvin and Herb leading the Circle City Stompers, a raucous clown band, through the streets of downtown. The parade grew larger and longer as we gathered up flocks of people waving Pacer flags, and we entered Market Square Arena triumphant, to a sold out crowd of 17,096.

Randy Foxworthy, always a good sport, wore a badge that read, "Eliz Kraft was right."

I was right about being able to sell out the arena only because I was bold and had a flock of sixty of the most talented marketing and event people sheltered under my wings.

20

THE WORLD'S BEST BUSINESS ADVICE

On Friday the thirteenth, January 1984, I was promoted to vice president, and Fred Simon called me down to his office.

"Congratulations, Eliz!" he said. "I have some advice that will ensure your success."

I leaned forward, eager to receive his wisdom.

"Never do anything that will cause you to close your door."

"All right," I replied, realizing that in all my years at Simon, I had only once encountered a closed door. Fred went back to his paperwork and seemed to forget I was there.

"Never do anything that will cause you to close your door." "If you can conduct all of your business with an open door, you don't have to worry about anything else."

"What else, Mr. Simon?" I asked.

"Nothing," he said. "If you can conduct all of your business with an open door, you don't have to worry about anything else."

"Thank you, Mr. Simon."

21

ALL-STAR GAME

No other team in the NBA had ever experienced the kind of surge in attendance that we were bringing to the Pacers. As a result, David Stern, then commissioner of the NBA, called Melvin and Herb to ask for a meeting. He wanted to discuss bringing the All-Star Game to Indianapolis.

"Bring your marketing guy," he said.

A week later when we walked into Stern's office, he greeted us but looked disappointed.

"I thought you were going to bring your guy."

"We did," Herb said. "This girl is our guy."

Having agreed to float the idea of an All-Star Game in Indianapolis, we called together the Pacer staff, the Commission for Downtown, and the Simon marketing and corporate relations staff. Teri Moore had come up with a bold strategy to market tickets. The plan was to hold the game in half the Hoosier Dome, which meant selling 45,000 seats. Most All-Star games were played in regular-sized arenas with less than 20,000 seats.

To sell out half the Hoosier Dome, we would run three double-page ads with coupons in *The Indianapolis Star* three Sundays in a row, plus radio spots. Coupons would be the only way to buy tickets. The idea was approved, and the newspaper ended up giving us a huge discount and became a sponsor. We sold out in four weeks, an all-time record of 43,000 tickets!

Vic Ruthig and his staff put together a razzle-dazzle pre-game show timed down to the second. First, West Point Cadets marched around the court, singing *The Star-Spangled Banner* as 50,000 balloons dropped from overhead. Next, a group of Olympic stars, including gymnast Mary Lou Retton, took to the court while an 18,000-person flashcard section covering the upper floor of the Hoosier Dome executed the grand finale. It was so fabulously magical, the crowd jumped to its feet, screaming and clapping!

> "Bring your marketing guy."
> "We did. This girl is our guy."

For Vic, the staff and me, the timing was very serious business because our show in the dome had to peak and close just moments before the NBA went live on TV. We were confident in our ability to time events to the millisecond. Vic even stopped eating sugar a week before a big event, swearing that being sugar-free gave him greater sensitivity to the passing seconds.

My staff and I had taken a calculated risk by hiring an intern to design the timing and sequences for the 18,000-person flashcard finale. Scott Givens was an engineering student at Purdue, and I was confident he could pull it off. He did a brilliant job for us and later formed a company that produces opening and closing ceremonies for the Olympics.

22

A MILLION DOLLAR SHOT

"Let's have a promotion for a million dollar basketball shot!"

Vic Ruthig and Jim Austin were shooting air balls in my office, trying to convince me to join their excitement over yet another halftime stunt for the Pacers.

"Okay, okay!" I relented. "Put a proposal together."

They came back with a small model of a contraption designed to be wheeled onto the basketball court. It looked like a wooden slingshot that David might have used to take down Goliath, except for the moving parts and wheels.

The plan was to pick a random person from the Pacer audience, have him put a basketball in the gizmo, and pull the lever. If he made a basket, he would win $1 million! Jim had found an insurance company willing to insure the stunt and pay out the million if necessary. We walked the plan over to the brothers who thought it was risky but agreed anyway. We were always trying to come up with ideas to add excitement to the game. Back then, the players weren't burning up the court like they do now.

My marketing department started creating publicity about the million dollar basket. Melvin and Herb asked every day how construction of the gizmo was coming along. When the magic ball shooter finally appeared, we rolled it out on the game floor, put the ball in place, and pulled the lever. The test ball whooshed across the arena, grazing the outside of the rim.

Perfect!

The morning before the game, I was informed the magic ball shooter was broken. Apparently, too many tryouts had snapped the lever, and no one could fix it. Melvin and Herb responded appropriately.

"You've really screwed up this time! You've embarrassed us!"

Back in my office, I gave the problem a lot of thought. The insurance company had reneged on the deal since the machine fouled out and was no longer part of the stunt. Suddenly a light glimmered in my frantic brain. I decided to ask the brothers to give us $1 million. It would only be out of the bank for three hours, and then we would put it right back because what random person in the crowd could sink a basket from center court?

I visualized a million $1 bills being brought from the bank to Market Square Arena by a police escort with flashing red lights and sirens. I could feel the awe of the crowd as the money was delivered! The publicity! The Six O'clock News! Top of the hour! Front page of *The Indianapolis Star*! I called Jim and Vic to my office to explain the new stunt.

"We'll make a spectacle of the money, but nobody will win it. No fan is going to make a basket from center court," I said. "It's fool proof!"

"No, no! Eliz!" They both started waving their arms. "Don't do it! This is Indiana. Every third person in the arena can make a basket from center court!"

I listened to them and made myself stop fantasizing. Jim went out and got a $5,000 sponsorship from a local bank to give away as a prize. The night of the game, a young man was picked at random from the crowd. He took his shot and, whoosh, nothing but net.

Holy crap!

23

BROTHERLY LOVE

All at once, Herb ran in through
the door on my left, jumped
over the coffee table, and ran
out the door to my right with
Melvin on his heels, screaming
and swinging at his head. I had
just started a lame explanation
about family dynamics when
the whole scene happened
again, this time right to left!

The *Sports Illustrated* reporters there to interview Melvin and Herb
looked at each other, and we all started howling with laughter.
Tears were still streaming down our faces when the brothers
walked into the room and introduced themselves as though
nothing unusual had happened.

Melvin and Herb together were fun to watch because they couldn't walk anywhere without constantly bumping into each other. Boing! Boing! Bump, bump. They were like magnets. I imagined their arms black and blue from banging into each other. And when they stopped and turned, instead of going in opposite directions, they frequently collided. They were the closest of brothers, each other's best friend and companion, even when they were fighting.

On this particular day, *Sports Illustrated* had sent writers to Indianapolis to interview the NBA's newest franchise owners. Their interview was to begin at 10:30 a.m.

At 11:15, Rodney had buzzed me on the intercom and said, "You better get upstairs because the brothers are fighting, and they haven't even started their interview."

I pulled out my tap shoes, grabbed my baton, and went up to the room that connected their offices. It was a private space used mostly for conversations between the brothers. I had just introduced myself, made sure the reporters had information on the company, and was telling them the Simons had been delayed by an important business deal when the chaos began.

I was sure the article was going to be a doozy one way or the other. The brothers were charming as individuals and irresistible as a team. Sure enough, in the article the writers dubbed Melvin and Herb the "Marx Brothers of Sports."

24

LITTLE BIRD

"Tell me the truth. What is your doctor saying?" Melvin asked.

I had hurt my back somewhere along the way and had severe pain in my hip. For several months I'd used crutches as doctors gave me different diagnoses. Concerned about my health, Melvin had called me into his office.

"My doctor thinks I should have a hip replacement," I said.

"Oh, no, kid! You can't do that. You're too young. You would have to have three of them in your lifetime."

"I know, but I don't know what to do."

"Let's call Sam LeFrak. He just had a hip replacement after trying a lot of other things first. Get Sam LeFrak on the phone," Melvin shouted out the door.

After he had Sam on the phone, Melvin told him about my hip pain and asked for advice.

"No, Sam, it's nothing like that. I've never touched her. She's like a little bird…"

At that point, I lost track of the conversation because it was pretty bizarre that Melvin Simon and Sam LeFrak, giants of the real estate world, were talking about my hip pain. To hear Melvin call me "a little bird" particularly boggled my mind.

On Sam's recommendation, Melvin sent me to two specialists in New York, who disagreed with each other, so subsequently, I was sent to the Pacer doctor in Indianapolis who solved my problem with a back brace.

Melvin cared about all his employees. One time, Jim Austin traveled with Melvin to Paris to visit Jacques Cousteau. Jim had a cold when he left Indianapolis and pneumonia when he returned. After a few days, Melvin called him at home to see how he was doing and if he needed anything. Even with his fortune, Melvin couldn't have bought the kind of loyalty he inspired with his nurturing.

25
1984

Advertising is the rattling of a stick inside a swill bucket.
—George Orwell

In 1984, before we got really busy, the Simon marketing department created and produced 3,034 different ads.

Among them were 653 radio commercials and 134 television spots; 1,445 newspaper ads, magazine covers, counter cards and signs; and 802 printed pieces devoted to specific malls for their grand openings.

As a totally in-house advertising department, we didn't just "rattle a stick," we made it dance!

It's incredible to look back on the tremendous amount of work we did without cell phones or computers. Just the other day, a few of us were talking about the time we had a fax machine installed. We thought it was a miracle!

26
THE WAY WE WERE

I was having a small meeting in the hotel lobby when the elevator door on the left opened. Inside were a small round table, two chairs, wine glasses, flowers, and two lit candles.

"How unusual," everyone said.

Then the elevator door on the right opened and an easy chair, slippers, a small skirted table with a lamp, a folded newspaper, and a lit cigarette in a deep ashtray came into view. Again everyone was startled.

I was neither surprised nor confused. My marketing team and I were in Virginia to open another mall, and some of them were sending me a message. They were tired, hungry and wanted my attention. I knew I had better wrap up the meeting and see what was going on before they sent down a toilet seat.

I got in the elevator with the easy chair, put on the slippers, opened the paper, and was smoking the cigarette when the door opened on the sixth floor.

"Hello," I said to my little band of mischief-makers. "Are you ready for dinner?"

My marketing staff was always the first to arrive at a mall for the grand opening and the last to leave. Sometimes they were on the road for weeks at a time. They stuck together, watched out for each other and me, and generally avoided the pitfalls of life on the road. So if every now and then they burned off energy by having a little fun at the hotel, I was ready to play along. During one mall opening, they decided to move the Coke machine to a different floor of the hotel every night. Each time, they left a sign saying where it had gone for the evening.

One of my all-time favorites was the hard roll caper. We were staying in a particularly dreary hotel where rock-hard dinner rolls were served with every meal. My staff began saving them. At breakfast on the last day, I noticed the tablecloth was littered with crumbs that seemed to be falling from overhead. I looked up and saw the light fixture over my table, adorned with hard rolls dangling and bumping together.

A less subtle message was sent to me when we were struggling to open Newport Centre. Walking through the marketing department, I saw a small white object floating overhead. It was hanging from the ceiling by transparent thread.

"What's that?" I asked.

Teri Moore glanced up and said, "Oh, that's Gostov."

"Gostov who?" I asked.

"Ghost-of-a-chance we're going make this mall happen," she said.

At that time, sixty-nine people worked in my different departments within marketing, which not only created but produced the advertising for over one hundred fifty existing malls, all development and leasing brochures, grand opening campaigns, our magazine, party invitations, television commercials, and leasing and development videos. Every now and then, we also created RFPs (request for proposals) from different cities, the occasional zoning argument, and helped Melvin write his speeches.

Our special events department handled groundbreaking ceremonies, grand openings, re-grand openings, mall events, parties and corporate entertaining. The mall decor group designed, purchased and installed the furnishings and decoration for grand openings, re-grand openings, a Christmas fantasy and Santa Claus land, corporate events, and the large offices we set up every year at the Las Vegas convention. A growing sponsorship area and new west coast marketing office filled out my roster.

At any given time, less than half my staff was in the home office because our work wasn't in Indianapolis. My coworkers could be scattered from Jersey City to Seattle to Topeka. With his special events and sponsorship duties, Jim Austin only spent fifty nights at home during one of our busiest years.

I had no idea where I might be going from one day to the next. In addition to all the mall work, eight or ten corporate officers plus my staff could tap me for a meeting at any time. I not only didn't know where I was going, sometimes I didn't know where I was. Try telling room service you're on the fourteenth floor of a hotel only six stories high.

"Oh, I'm sorry. That must have been yesterday."

But even chaos can become routine, and with discipline, patterns emerge. My secretary, JoAnne Hancock, organized my time and resources, and my day planner was stuffed with plane tickets. The routine for traveling with my staff was that until we had to fasten our seat belts to land, we were discussing projects in general and strategy for the upcoming meeting. That always worked until the day Vic and I were about to land in New York.

"So, Eliz, what's this meeting about?" Vic asked.

"Vic! I am here for you. It's your meeting!"

"No, Eliz. It's yours."

Neither one of us had any idea why we were going to New York, why we had gotten up at five a.m., or who I was going to kill as soon as we landed. We sat in La Guardia, waiting for the home office to open, then Vic went to a pay phone to call JoAnne. She said our partners at A & S Plaza had called an emergency meeting, and she had forgotten to mention it.

All the other Simon VPs had wives to run their homes, cook dinner, and pack their clothes. JoAnne took over paying my bills after the time I was gone so long for back-to-back mall openings that the utility company turned off the water in my house. JoAnne later represented me in the purchase of a new home. When I traveled, she always phoned me late in the evening with updates and reports on any of my staff who was also traveling.

Ours was a well-oiled machine, and in twelve years and almost twenty-five million square feet of shopping centers, I only missed one plane. At the airport my cab driver could not open his trunk to get my luggage out. After much back and forth, he insisted we go to his neighborhood to get tools to open the trunk. The porter waiting to take my luggage urged me not to go, to forget the luggage, and just get on the plane.

"You are a beautiful little white girl, and nobody ain't never going to see you again," he said.

We embraced like family when I made it back to the airport two hours later and took the next flight out.

27

GERALD PAUL

One day I received a luncheon invitation from Gerald Paul, the president of Paul Harris Stores and a legend in the retail world. In preparation for the meeting, I familiarized myself with all the malls that contained his stores. Only then did I realize his stores numbered in the hundreds.

In 1954, Gerald Paul and Earl Harris opened their first store in a small strip center in Indiana. They installed air conditioning and kept the store open evening hours, innovative ideas at the time. Gerald continued his creative and innovative approach throughout the lifetime of his stores, using research to determine the direction of his private label merchandise.

At lunch, Gerald told fascinating stories of trial and error in the retail business. I said that at Madigan's, we always felt his stores were our biggest competition. His store windows were the ones that attracted the most attention in the malls, not because he was spending a fortune on creating works of art like we were, but because his logo—the silhouette of a woman's face in vibrant colors—commanded attention from a distance.

Gerald then said he wanted to put someone with extensive retail experience on his board of directors, and Herb Simon had recommended me.

"I don't think I'm a good candidate," I said. "I only have a high school diploma."

Gerald said Herb had told him I was the kind of smart that wasn't taught in school, and Gerald's own background allowed him to see the possibilities in people like me. He had fled the Nazis at the age of thirteen and arrived in America, speaking little English. Nonetheless, he'd graduated from high school two years later. He was self-taught and self-disciplined, a man who, through bold and courageous action and initiatives, had built a retail empire.

At my first board meeting, I met Gerald's business partner Earl Harris; Gene Step from Eli Lilly; Allen Boorstein, president of Amber Blocks; and Tomio Taki, head of Takihyo, which held a controlling interest in the Anne Klein Group and, later, Donna Karan. As a board member, I got a graduate degree in management, leadership and personal style. Even after I rotated off the board and to this day, Gerald and his wife Dorit are treasured friends, as is Tomio Taki.

Gerald and Dorit are also respected art collectors. Both art museums in Indianapolis have wings bearing their names. On one occasion, I asked Gerald what I should look for and what should be my criteria for my own small art collection. He surprised me by saying, "Never buy a work of art that you can afford. You'll tire of it."

That was just one of the many life lessons Gerald taught me.

As I drove to his board meetings, I encouraged myself not to be intimidated by the learned, experienced men sitting around me. I learned that my raw common sense and problem solving abilities made me a valued member of the board.

28

A HISTORIC OPENING

On February 11, 1861, President-elect Abraham Lincoln passed through Indianapolis on his way from Illinois to Washington, DC. That day, he addressed Indianapolis residents at the Bates House Hotel on the corner of Washington and Illinois Streets.

On that same site, February 16, 1985, the new Simon-owned Embassy Suites Hotel was ready for guests. For its grand opening, we decided to replicate the events surrounding Lincoln's historic appearance in Indianapolis.

The weekend was called Suite Memories of the 1860s, for which we did extensive research into entertaining of the period.

We were surprised by the heavy seven-course meals served back then, and we couldn't figure out where the masses of flowers in photographs of Lincoln's visit had been found. We had to make a few adjustments. To accommodate the modern appetite, we reduced the dinner to four courses. The flowers, we had flown in from Hawaii.

Elaborate invitations were sent to Simon business associates and friends, asking them to join us for an overnight trip back in time and to dress in costumes typical of the 1800s. The hotel was filled to capacity. Our guests moved from high tea to cocktails with a Stephen Foster impersonator at the piano. Given an hour to dress for the banquet and the presidential reception, our guests transformed themselves into statesmen, officers, and ladies of the manor in exquisite ball gowns.

Abraham Lincoln played by actor Richard Blake, Indiana Governor Robert Orr, Mayor William H. Hudnut, and the Simons led the grand march to the Presidential Ball. Dance instructors taught the waltz and quickstep to adventurous couples. Mark Twain and Louisa May Alcott impersonators told stories and read aloud, a minstrel show was performed, historian Dillon Bustin presented a repertoire of President Lincoln's favorite songs, and the Don't Tread on Me Dance troupe traced the history of American step dancing. The next morning, an exact copy of the newspaper printed on February 12, 1861, lay outside each hotel room door.

Time travel, indeed.

With overnight guests out by 11 a.m., the hotel opened to the public at noon. A full page ad in *The Indianapolis Star* had invited the public to tour the hotel and enjoy the same entertainment we'd presented the night before. Moments after we opened the doors, the fire marshall showed up, concerned about crowd control. Almost twenty-five thousand people had lined up around the block, waiting to see the hotel.

The last of our guests didn't leave until dusk. Instead of being tired, I felt energized by the crowd and the response we received every time we had an opportunity to work in Indianapolis. I wished more and more that we could open a mall at home.

29

MEL AND HERB'S CLUB

The brothers wanted to do something special to celebrate their twenty-fifth year in business. That spring the International Council of Shopping Centers annual convention was to be held in New Orleans.

Instead of leasing space inside the convention center as usual, the brothers wanted us to find a unique place to set up the Simon booth.

Rodney Putz and I flew down to New Orleans to look at some options and found a storefront for rent at Convention Center Boulevard and Julia Street, kitty-corner from the convention. Rodney thought the space would work just fine, but I said it was way too small, and we would need to rent the warehouse behind the store as well.

"Why would we ever need that much room?" he asked.

"Because we're going to open a nightclub," I said.

We rented both spaces, broke through the back wall of the store into the warehouse, and set up conference rooms and leasing offices. In the storefront we built a bar called Mel and Herb's Club, modeled after Harlem's Cotton Club. Neon signs were designed and installed above the bar. The Mel and Herb's Club logo was printed on menus, ashtrays and leasing collateral.

By day, we operated the venue as our leasing suite. By night, we were the hottest jazz club in the city. Jazz legend Al Hirt was our star attraction. The place was packed, and the joint was jumpin'! Mel and Herb's Club had the shortest run of any nightclub anywhere—only two and a half days. But afterward, our business associates talked about it for years.

I thought those were my glory days. From creating a historical pageant at the Embassy Suites to producing a nightclub, I felt fulfilled, satisfied and appreciated. I could have folded my tent, watered the animals, and moved on to the Marketing Circus in the sky.

But, no, there was more to come.

30

IT'S THE PEOPLE

"Melvin Simon & Associates is not the number of malls built or the amount of GLA (gross leasable area) generated over the last twenty-five years; it is the people who have wrestled with challenges and won, labored and laughed, dreamed and dared over the years."

—Melvin and Herb on the twenty-fifth anniversary of Melvin Simon & Associates

31

MEET ME IN ST. LOUIS

It was approaching midnight, and I was alone in a hotel suite with somebody else's husband.

He slid closer to me on the couch and took my hand. The man making me a little nervous was Bob Hope.

That day, August 8, 1985, we had opened St. Louis Centre, the nation's largest enclosed downtown shopping mall at the time. It contained 6 million pounds of steel, 14,000 cubic yards of concrete, and a humongous glass roof that shed light into the arcade between Dillard's and Famous-Barr. The nearby skyscrapers were visible through the roof, adding to the urban vibe of this dazzling new center.

When we started the project, we knew something special was needed for our first downtown opening, and the developer, Jerry Garvey, suggested Bob Hope. We thought maybe, just maybe, Mr. Hope might be intrigued by our efforts to revitalize the great American city of St. Louis.

I got a phone number for what I assumed was Mr. Hope's agent. After the second ring, a familiar voice said, "Bob Hope here."

Holy crap! Bob Hope! A living legend! The movie star! The guy who entertained the troops at Christmas! I managed to croak out a few words about St. Louis and our new downtown mall. He was interested in urban renewal and said he would check his schedule.

Two days later, my secretary said some clown claiming to be Bob Hope had called twice. I phoned back immediately to learn that Mr. Hope had an engagement in Canada right before we needed him in St. Louis…but…if we could send a plane for him, he would be happy to come to St. Louis.

A plane? No problem!

Our opening day was seven weeks away, during which time Mr. Hope called regularly to check on the mall's progress. He said he thought we were making a valiant effort, and he would

> Bob Hope took my hand, leaned over and...

be a booster for our cause. Mr. Hope phoned again the day before leaving Canada and asked if I would come up on the jet and fly back with him to St. Louis. I really wanted to, but I had too much work to do in the mall. We agreed to meet at the mall and attend the VIP dinner party together, then go to the ribbon cutting in the morning. I assumed he wanted me with him because he was hard of hearing and needed a companion with a loud voice.

August 8 brought full sun and humidity to St. Louis. Mr. Hope welcomed the immense crowd that had gathered to watch Melvin and Herb Simon, Jerry Garvey, Bill Dillard, May Company executives, and the mayor cut the ceremonial ribbon. As the ribbon fell to the ground, dozens of six-foot helium balloons lifted a thirty-foot blue and white archway far above the mall's entrance. Hundreds of red heart-shaped balloons filled the archway. And there was more—10,000 red Mylar helium balloons ascended into the bright blue sky as 8,000 white air-filled balloons drifted to the ground! Did I mention the flag waving and the marching band? That was followed by photo opportunities, lunch, media interviews, and a mall appearance before dinner.

As we rode in a limo back to the hotel, Bob (he was Bob by then) asked if I would come up to his suite. In his rooms he told me to make myself comfortable while he changed clothes. He reappeared, wearing a cardigan. I'd seen a silver box about eight inches tall with a ribbon on the coffee table. It was a gift for me. Bob said he found it in Canada and was reminded of my quest for downtown St. Louis. I opened the box and inside was a Royal Dalton mug of Don Quixote!

Then one of my life's most beautiful moments occurred. Thinking about it, I still get goose bumps to this day. Bob Hope took my hand, leaned over and sang. He sang a song that he made famous.

"Thanks for the memories...."

32

ON THE PATIO

The Simons were sitting shiva after the death of a family member. Having been raised Catholic, I had a limited understanding of the Jewish religion.

All I knew was that I needed to show up at the house and bring food. I was sitting on a sofa in the living room when the men got up and went out to the patio.

"We need one more," Melvin shouted.

"What are they doing?" I asked.

"They're going to pray," someone said.

I thought that was a good idea, so I got up and joined the men on the patio. I believe the group included all three brothers,

"Oh, let her stay. She's got more balls than all of us put together."

Dr. Mason Goodman, Tom Shine, Irv Katz, and some others. Then I realized something was wrong. I could feel tension all around me. Everyone seemed uncomfortable, and no one was saying the prayers.

Then Melvin said, "Oh, let her stay. She's got more balls than all of us put together."

"Baruch atah Adonai…"

33

IN THE MIDDLE
RING—HERB'S OFFICE

Herb's office was the epicenter of the business, and if Herb was in town, the vice presidents gathered there at the end of the day to have a drink and swap stories.

Those early evenings were relaxed and congenial, a remarkable contrast from work hours.

From nine to five, that same office functioned like traffic control at a major airport. Four chairs sat lined up in front of Herb's desk, with a constant stream of people waiting to see him, report on progress or delays, look at budgets, ask questions, and seek advice. Herb saw people on a first-come, first-serve basis unless Melvin or Jerry Gershman entered the room, then he took precedence over everyone else.

The Simon family had a totally transparent, open-door way of doing business. We all knew what projects were underway.

We sat and waited our turns together, consequently, anyone could listen in on anyone else's progress report, problem or question. Leasing guys, development officers, marketing staff, accountant or lawyer, Herb handled everyone in the same way. Without notes. He could move from one project to the next and still manage a steady stream of phone calls from outside the office. All day, every day, without hesitation or confusion.

"What's next?" he asked again and again.

After we got our answers, we peeled off and were replaced by the next group of supplicants. Sometimes community leaders showed up to plead for donations. If the request was extraordinary, such as money to produce the Pan Am Games, Herb called me.

"Listen," he'd say, "we need to raise a lot of money, so I'm going to get everybody together and ask for donations. You pledge $10,000 dollars, and I'll cover you. The guys always feel they have to donate more than you."

The strategy worked every time.

The open-door environment in Herb's office also presented new challenges. Sometimes I felt as if I had prepared to be a juggler in a side ring at the circus but suddenly found myself blinded by the spotlight in the middle ring. I never knew if I should tame the lions or ride the elephant.

I learned to think on my feet and speak my mind in any and all situations. No time for anxiety or hurt feelings. Meetings could boil over and turn into a street fight or a family feud. Sometimes, the meeting stopped when a sports celebrity or a national politician walked in. You never knew who might strut through Herb's door.

One day, several of us were called to Herb's office to see a model of the proposed garage for the Westin Indianapolis. It was an ugly three- or four-story cement block building directly in front of the hotel. Everyone smiled and nodded agreeably as if the eyesore were just dandy. All at once Melvin rushed in, glanced at it, ripped off the garage, and threw it on the floor.

"What the hell is the matter with you?" he yelled, heading for the door. "Don't you know buildings have to breathe? Put that damn thing underground!"

The Capital Improvement Board subsequently built a lush green park on top of the garage. That was the first time I thought... that's why he is Melvin Simon and we are not.

"Look, why don't we all stand up, beat the hell out of him, and get it over with!"

Sometimes during a meeting, Herb's driver made an appearance. Willie was a good-natured, good-looking guy often dispatched on errands then left to his own course of action. One afternoon he walked in, looking happier than usual with himself. He'd been asked to take food and money to a family in need.

"They were grateful and said they would pray for you," he reported to Herb.

"How did they know the gifts were from me?" Herb asked. "I told you not to tell them."

Willie said he had done exactly as instructed and had announced the food and money were anonymous gifts from Mr. Herb Simon.

Another time Willie reported back, carrying a brown paper lunch bag. He bounded into the office, holding the bag in a death grip out in front of him, and strided right up to Herb's desk as if his task were more important than any of ours. With a flourish he scattered the contents of the bag out on the desk.

Glittering diamonds rolled over paperwork, dropped into open binders, and skittered around the ashtray. Rounds, emerald cuts, square and oblong diamonds, all different cuts but only one size. Enormous. His desk was ablaze! I wanted to reach out my hands and spread the gems into a thin coating of priceless light. I wanted to roll them like dice. I wanted to smell them, hold them, taste them.

Instead, I left the room.

Given the high-stakes atmosphere, Herb was unusually even-tempered. Twice, he got furious with me but never raised his voice. Through the calm, I saw an unmistakable steely, ice blue anger and knew I was in real trouble. Yet he let me fight for my ideas and explain the thinking that had led to my choices.

The most enraged I ever saw Herb was the time a development VP lost a zoning battle. Herb did not acknowledge him for days. He refused to speak or look at him. The man simply didn't exist. If Herb wouldn't recognize his presence, how could we? Everyone had to ignore him.

Finally I spoke up. "Look, why don't we all stand up, beat the hell out of him, and get it over with!"

The tension was broken, and we all laughed. Then I mentioned that maybe a zoning battle was a marketing job, earning myself another area of responsibility.

Herb gave us a lot of freedom in producing our elaborate marketing stunts and events.

Most of our ideas involved degrees of risk, but risk was accepted, even expected, at Simon. Risk was part of doing business at the speed the company moved, and an element in the Simon brothers' extraordinary success. Herb told us not to let a failure stop us from coming up with big ideas.

"Herb, we want to have a huge parade from our offices to Market Square Arena on the Pacers opening night..."

"Herb, we want to suspend twelve-foot butterflies for the opening of East Towne Mall..."

"Herb, we want to shoot lasers just above head level at Ross Park..."

"Herb, we want to produce the world's longest ribbon cutting..."

"Herb, we want...we want...we want..."

He would always listen and ask, "How much?" He might question our reasoning and methodology, then send us off, saying, "Don't embarrass me. God bless you."

On the other hand, when the marketing department had finished a corporate brochure, video, or development or leasing materials and I needed to get them approved, the meeting became more than a presentation. It was a competition about who had the most power or who was most in favor that day. Because marketing materials were openly discussed and debated by every officer in the corporation, we had to meet in the conference room. My audience was fluid, and the crowd might turn over two or three times, with no one seeing a complete presentation. Don would have to take a phone call, Poetz leave to catch a plane, and Irv and June rush to an early lunch...

I typically concluded my comments then waited for final reactions from anyone left in the room, which could be interesting if that included the coffee guy or someone's driver. When Herb and Melvin loved the materials, we were okay. If either of them showed the slightest negative reaction, then blood was in the water, and everybody turned on Marketing like restless sharks. Marketing, like art, was subjective and nobody had the same opinion.

But I had a secret weapon. As I was being sucked into the vortex, I held up three fingers to my creative director, Deb Coons, which meant GO GET GERSHMAN! Jerry Gershman was the executive VP over development. Deb ran out of the room, careening around corners to reach Jerry's office. He was always on the phone, so she couldn't scream, "Marketing is being butchered in the conference room!" She had to pantomime being strangled to signal the desperate situation.

Moments later, Jerry strolled into the conference room, putting a fresh stick of gum in his mouth. Quiet, graceful, intense, his presence changed the room. He stabilized the group because he didn't condone the high drama that often comes with a high-risk, high-reward environment. Order was restored. Marketing would be allowed back in the safety of the boat, and we would survive to swim with the sharks another day.

34

THE SCARS

Sometime during my third year at Simon, I became uncomfortable with the many scars and broken blood vessels on my face and body.

I was so used to covering myself with makeup that I'd almost forgotten I was still wearing the external symbols of my childhood abuse.

Even now, when a new doctor or dentist looks at my X-rays, he or she asks in one way or another, "What the hell happened to you?"

My deep, inner scars were not visible, not even on an X-ray.

Finally, I decided to save money to have the scars and broken capillaries removed. Beginning the procedures forced me to acknowledge and explain to the doctor what had happened. This was a turning point for me because I realized that I no longer had a reason to be ashamed or embarrassed. What had happened was not my fault, and the shame was not mine.

Kevin O'Keefe was one of my most trusted staff members. I confided to him, "I'm going to start going to a doctor to remove marks from when my mother used to beat me. I was hoping you would come with me the first time."

"Alrighty then, would you like to leave now?" he said.

35

BECOMING A HOOSIER

Three achievements are particularly precious in the state of Indiana: a blue ribbon at the Indiana State Fair, a pace car from the Indianapolis 500, and a Sagamore of the Wabash Award bestowed by the governor.

In the late 1980s, I was invited to be a director of the 500 Festival and given a pace car to drive during the months of April and May, to advertise the Memorial Day weekend Indianapolis 500 race. My first pace car was a white Pontiac Trans Am convertible decorated with shocking pink race decals. The engine roared and screamed when I touched the accelerator.

It was a balmy, spring night when I drove the pace car home for the first time. Revving the engine and making a tremendous ruckus, I drove the car up and down my block and took a couple of spins around my circular driveway, causing my neighbors to start streaming out of their homes. Did I mention the honking and waving?

First the kids came outside, then the men and women. Because I traveled so much, I only barely knew my neighbors. There was a lot of laughter and excitement with neighbors running home to get their cameras. The whole neighborhood took pictures of themselves sitting in the pace car and stayed out after dark, talking about growing up in Indiana and never missing the Indianapolis 500.

Everyone had a story to tell about race day traditions. It was the fathers who organized race day for the family, decided who was old enough to go, what food should be taken, what time they would leave the house, and most importantly, the route they had to take to the track. I heard about everyone's favorite driver, rides some of them had taken in other pace cars, and race day stories generations old.

When we all finally went home that night, I had the impression everybody felt a little better about the world and our place in it. We felt closer as neighbors because I had brought to our neighborhood a highly esteemed Indiana tradition. From that night on, the pace car never went into the garage until long after dark, and it never went to the carwash without the little boys next door, riding along and always praying, as I did, that someone they knew would see us.

Next, I set my heart on winning a blue ribbon at the Indiana State Fair. Inspired by the exquisite miniature Thorne Rooms in the Art Institute in Chicago, I made a hobby of building and furnishing doll houses. I bought doll house kits, built them, painted and wallpapered them, installed wood floors, crown moldings and chandeliers. Then I bought miniature furniture and dolls to create happy families. Along the way, I also designed and built miniature stores. After completing a difficult antique store, I entered it in competition at the fairgrounds and won a blue ribbon, plus $25!

I tell about the pace car and blue ribbon with great pride, but I am most humbled by the Sagamore of the Wabash Award I received from Governor Frank O'Bannon. This award is given to honorees for their significant contributions to life in Indiana. I may not have been born a Hoosier, but I have participated fully, and still do all I can to deserve to live here.

My mother,
Francis Lorraine Carroll Kraft

My father,
Joseph Charles Kraft

My sisters, Laura, Ethel & Liane

Elizabeth Jo Kraft

Childhood home: 5450 W Madison, Chicago, IL

My sister, Laura, posing with the garbage cans

Al Hirt

Short Term Lease a Big Hit in New Orleans

It may have been the shortest-lived night club in history. Actually, it was planned that way. Mel & Herb's Club opened on a Wednesday and closed two days later, when the ICSC leasing convention ended. "This is what you do when you need more space," said Elizabeth Kraft, Vice

President of Marketing. "You go next door to the convention center, lease an old storefront. You turn it into leasing suites with a place to relax and enjoy friends."

One of the friends was Al Hirt who entertained the crowds with his brand of New Orleans jazz.

Leasing in New Orleans?
Don't miss Mel & Herb's!

The night I met
the 3 brothers

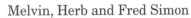
Melvin, Herb and Fred Simon

**The Personality of
Melvin Simon and Associates** *

Melvin and Herb Simon *

Melvin Simon with portrait *
of his father

Internal awards I passed out

*Herb Simon with most of the Vice Presidents

Jerry
Garvey

Jerry
Gershman

Suited up for
another meeting

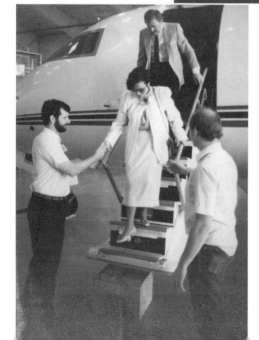

My office

MELVIN SIMON & ASSOCIATES, INC.

MEMORANDUM

TO: All Officers and Department Heads (please

FROM: Herbert Simon

DATE: March 23, 1989

SUBJECT: PROMOTION

I am pleased to announce that **Elizabeth Kraft**, Vice President of Marketing, is being promoted to **Senior Vice President of Melvin Simon & Associates, Inc.**, responsible for Marketing. This promotion is effective immediately.

This promotion reflects Eliz's continuing success at associating Simon with marketing excellence, a process that began when she joined our company in 1981. It is also consistent with our re-alignment and establishment of executive management responsibilities for our **parent company and the development and management subsidiaries.**

Please join me in congratulating Eliz Kraft, Senior Vice President-Marketing.

/ m c

FUN DINNER DANCING ENTERTAINMENT SURPRISES

THE
MOVING
PICTURE
BALL

HONORING
STEVEN SPIELBERG

Kevin O'Keefe, me, Billie Scott & Deb Coons

Going to the ball in Hollywood

Larry Conrad and me opening the Indiana Roof

Embassy Suites opening

Lt. Governor John Mutz, Herb Simon, "Abe Lincoln",
Governor Orr, Mayor Hudnut, & Melvin Simon   *

Diana Dietsch, Deb Coons
& Teri Moore

Michael Moriarty and me

Robert Saylers,
Pacer President
Herb and Mel Simon *

**Indiana Pacers
and Indianapolis
host record NBA
All-Star Game.**

by Teri Moore, Marketing

PACER
PRIDE

INDIANA
PACERS

Larry Bird

Unfurling the flag on the Embassy Suites Hotel

Billie Scott, Bob Hope and me

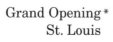

One of many phone
messages and a gift
from Bob Hope

Grand Opening *
St. Louis

Vic Ruthig, Jim Austin and me

Rod Putz and me

Bears' Jim McMahon at Markland

According to the census, the population of Kokomo, Indiana is 47,808. According to the estimates, 40,000 of them came to the town's Markland Mall to see Chicago Bears' star **Jim McMahon.** The event was the celebration of the center's reopening after expansion and extensive renovation.

"I didn't know this kind of crowd was in store when I agreed to come to Kokomo," said the charismatic quarterback. Mall manager **Jim Lundgren** said that McMahon signed more than 5,000 autographs.

ROB BANAYOT

Treasures from the "Kermitage Collection"

Muppet creator Jim Henson is working with MSA to bring "Miss Piggy's Art Treasures" to several Simon malls. The exclusive promotion features take-offs of such Old Masters' works as Auguste Rodin's *The Kiss*, re-interpreted Muppet-style as *The Smooch*.

"Miss Piggy's Art Treasures" opened at Greenwood Park Mall in suburban Indianapolis in September and was part of the recent Claypool Court grand opening downtown. It is scheduled for St. Louis Centre as well as Simon properties in Texas before moving to the East Coast.

Many of the centers will capitalize on the "Muppetopolis" theme, highlighting the artwork, while including interactive video for children and other Muppet-related events.

Among the 12 paintings and two sculptures are such treasures as *Mona Piggy* and *Arisfroggle Contemplating the Bust of a Twerp.*

ROB BANAYOT

Mona Piggy

An Extraordinary Evening

MAXI Night 1983 was truly an Extraordinary Evening. I feel very strongly about the meaning of MAXI and want to share with you the crux of my speech from MAXI Night, October 1, 1983.

"Tonight is about marketing—the good, the better and the best. Marketing, to me, is the gentle art of friendly persuasion. Marketing is the idea which causes the spark, which creates the desire, which closes the sale. Marketing is power. . .it's harnessed creative energy."

"All of us have known that magic moment when we've been seized by the *good idea*. The moment when a thought. . .so strong, so clear, so right. . .has obsessed us. Leaving us grabbing our heads, breathless with our *own* brilliance. We've known the commitment, the dedication and that frighteningly furious dance of self-promotion it's taken to sell that idea. The worry, the pain, the anxiety and most of all, the exposure. It's hard to stay calm when your heart *and* your guts are involved. Your idea *must* be born. You *must* have approval and you *must* have the budget. There is no compromise. . .no second best. . .there is only getting the idea into production."

"It's those ideas. . .the stunners. . .that make management afraid for our mental health. We rush in, clutching our video tape, sign or marketing plan and they don't understand the *passion*. But that's okay, because it's those *same* ideas that bring us here tonight."

"Tonight is about ideas that brought us goose bumps. . .that surprised even us. . .that took our breath away. Tonight is a toast to MAXI, to the spirit of competition and the celebration of our talents and industry. Tonight, with the MAXI Awards, we honor each other for the idea, the sell, the production, the traffic in the malls and the ringing of the cash register."

"Tonight is about ideas that brought us goose bumps. . .that surprised even us. . .that took our breath away."

Eliz Kraft
Director of Marketing

It was, indeed, an honor to have served as 1983 MAXI Chairman. . .an honor to represent the industry, our Corporation and you.

paul harris

Gerald Paul and me

Creative Marketing

by Elizabeth J. Kraft
Vice President of Marketing

How does it happen? Was the famous "where's the beef?" ad the product of a single creative genius? When the popular Levi's 501 Blues commercials came to be, was someone sitting next to a window, staring out at the clouds when the idea miraculously struck?

Many of us have that idea about marketing. It's somehow mystical, or worse, arbitrary. Artists just sit around making pretty pictures. Writers wait for the magic light to strike. And it's all just a lot of

Sometimes fact of the ma work. Wendy ong before th created. The against a gia ould outspe They had to lienating p hemselves ounteratta re their t ontinuity roduct-o eated.

What th e beef?" single cr e merely ompetiti refully th loca the ha at. Th

What arketi phaza sines

Me, Deb Coons, Shari Simon & Jeff Cross at the ICSC Maxi Awards

Eliz Kraft

— THE SIMON NOTEBOOK —

17 years of MAXI

Since the International Council of Shopping Centers (ICSC) established the MAXI awards program in 1972, Simon has received 42 top-place honors over the years. Having won seven of her own MAXIs, Elizabeth J. Kraft, senior vice president of marketing, had this to say. "I think it's been a true team effort. None of the awards or accolades would be possible if it wasn't for the people I work for and the people who work for me."

This year's MAXIs went to the leasing brochure for Mall of America, and to Anderson Mall (Merchant Motivation Program). Six merits were received as well.

Mall of America

Simon Sweeps MAXI Awards

DEBBIE COONS

Eliz Kraft at the MAXI's with some of the celebrants.

MSA swept MAXI night at the ICSC's Fall Shopping Center Convention in Anaheim, picking up more of the international awards than any developer in the competition's history.

"Thank God," said Elizabeth Kraft, Vice President of Marketing. "I was told not to come home without one." Instead, MSA received a total of seven MAXI's and six Merit Awards.

"We've worked toward this for a number of years," she said. "And this shows we're going in the right direction. We've had strong leadership from Rodney Putz and I want to thank the creative geniuses I work for, who have a clear commitment to marketing. It also shows powerful support and originality from the malls."

About the Mel & Herb's Club Maxi, Kraft said the Marketing Department "wanted to share the award with Public Relations and Technical Services, without whose help this would have been impossible."

MSA's other Maxi's included the Pentagon City leasing brochure, the "Sell Star" motivation program, "Week for Women" at Midland Park Mall, "Rock 'N Video" at Northeast Mall,

Mayor Stephen Goldsmith

Winning $25 and a blue ribbon for miniature house

Photo by Squier Neal

Indianapolis 500

Helping Her Look Like a Million

Melvin Simon & Associate launched a 13-mall Statue of Liberty promotion to help raise the $230,000,000 needed for the restoration of the grand old lady during he 100th anniversary.

"We wanted to salute our nation's international heritag during this special year," said Vic Ruthig, Manager o Promotions and Merchandi ing. "It's a real birthday celebration."

Thousands of dollars hav already been raised at Sime malls throughout the count with a touring exhibit whic highlights both a 30-foot in flatable replica and an 8 x foot jigsaw puzzle of the Ellis Island statue.

Dr. William Meek   Stephen Taylor

Friends preparing for Mall of America

* From *Simon Developments* magazine

36

"Paging Elizabeth Kraft! Paging Elizabeth Kraft!"

Before cell phones, it was not unusual to be paged at an airport. I left the gate and found a phone to answer the page.

"Melvin wants to speak to you," a secretary said in my ear. Her voice had the special tone that meant, "Brace yourself."

And then Melvin bellowed, "Are you stealing from me? I hear you're stealing from me!"

"Melvin, why would I steal from you? I work for you, you pay me every two weeks. We're even."

"They say you're stealing from me."

When working for a family business, any sentence that begins with "They say…" is a minefield. "They" will always have more credibility and more access than any employee. And the larger the family, the more you will hear from "they." Having started my working life in a family-owned business, Madigan's, I had learned to give answers that were as preposterous as the questions.

"Okay, fine, Melvin. Let's think about this. Are all the planes still accounted for?" I asked.

"Yes," he said.

"Are all the regional malls still there?"

"Yes."

"Really, Melvin, would I steal anything else?"

"You're right, kid. Never mind."

I went back to gate 7A.

37

A SEAGULL STORY

Once during a trip to California, some coworkers and I were having dinner in a restaurant on a pier extending into the ocean.

About a dozen tourists were feeding the seagulls, throwing bread up in the air for them.

I noticed two groups of birds. The larger group was flying in circles as if performing a graceful ballet. They seemed to understand the timing of the bread being thrown. As a piece flew up, one of the gulls swooped out of the circle to snatch the bread. Next throw, next seagull, swoop, get bread. On and on it went. The birds were flying, taking turns, catching bread, and entertaining the tourists.

The second group was the screamers. They stayed in the water and bobbed along. Not much bread fell to them, so they were screaming as only seagulls can. The more bread the flying birds caught, the more the lazy ones screamed.

Some things are universal.

38

A RESTAURANT IN CHICAGO

About ten Simon employees had been summoned to dinner with development partners in Chicago. I had no idea why I was there, but I knew I would be expected to speak knowledgeably when Melvin gave me the cue.

He was directing a conversation about developing and managing hotels, but I wasn't paying much attention because I'd never been involved with hotels. I expected to be asked about something else later in the conversation.

All of a sudden, Melvin looked at me and pointed, saying, "Okay, we'll build the hotel, and she'll keep it over eighty percent occupied."

Baffled, I smiled and nodded as if that were a legitimate possibility.

Later, as he was leaving, I said, "Wait, Melvin. I don't know anything about marketing hotels."

Patting my shoulder, his eyes dancing, and his face in a wide grin, he said, "That's okay, Eliz. I don't know anything about building them."

That's how Melvin and Herb empowered people. Melvin knew that before the deal was done, I would know everything I needed to fulfill his promise.

39

THE 172-MILE CAB RIDE

I left the office, carrying an incredibly small but sensational evening bag containing a $100 bill and a tube of lipstick

After a typically long workday, Melvin, Jerry Gershman, Randy Foxworthy, two or three others, and I schlepped to our cars and drove to the airport. We were taking Melvin's plane to Chicago to attend a Christmas party being thrown by our development partners, Joe Beale and Associates. We planned to spend two hours at the party then fly back to Indianapolis.

At the party I noticed Melvin spending most of his time on the phone. After hanging up, he called me aside and told me the Gimbels' building in New York had come up for sale, and he and the other guys were leaving for New York immediately. They would stay in the Simon New York condo, but there was no room for me. They dropped me at the Chicago condo to spend the night and catch a commercial flight home the next morning.

Plans changed all the time if Melvin was involved, so I didn't think anything about it. I had been at Simon long enough to understand that a perceived opportunity was the driving force of daily life. No workday had any resemblance to the one before it, so this particular shenanigan was just another bump in the road. My biggest worry was how I was going to look in the morning.

At the airport the next day, the outfit that was so fabulous the night before looked outrageous in the early morning light. The plane to Indianapolis was filled with businessmen, which made me feel even more ridiculous in my party getup. When we got close to Indianapolis, the pilot kept circling because of fog. He finally announced that we would have to land in Evansville.

Evansville? I had never heard of Evansville. Evansville, Indiana? Evansville, Kentucky? Missouri? I had no clue.

After we landed, the businessmen crammed themselves into the three rental cars available in Evansville. I had only $27 dollars left after paying for the taxi to O'Hare Airport in Chicago. A ticket agent in Evansville told me a bus to Indianapolis was leaving later in the day, but the ticket cost more than $27. I had left home on a million dollar jet but couldn't afford to get back on a bus! I went outside and walked over to the first cab in line.

"Take me to Indianapolis," I said as if I were in full control of the situation.

The driver jumped out and started yelling that I was crazy. Other cab drivers gathered around to hear what the commotion was about. They all agreed that I must be insane. Apparently, no one had ever landed in Evansville and asked for a cab to drive the 172 miles to Indianapolis.

"It will cost you hundreds of dollars to get to Indianapolis!" one of the drivers said.

Getting one of those guys to drive me to Indy was my only hope, so I started to negotiate.

"I'll pay you whatever you want," I offered. I saw a glimmer of light in some of their eyes.

Finally, one of them said he might drive if I gave him $350 up front. I clutched my evening bag. The jig was up.

"I only have $27 right now, but when we get to Indianapolis, I'll be able to pay whatever you want," I said.

They were not convinced, so I tried demonstrating that money was no object for me.

"Look, my coat is genuine pink fur, and my bag is very expensive. It cost six hundred dollars," I said.

Those things seemed to be further proof that I was crazy.

I finally said, "Okay, listen to me. This is going to be an adventure! Has anyone else ever asked to be driven to Indianapolis? This is your chance for a very unusual day! Come on! Do something different for once. You'll be able to tell this story for years! Doesn't one of you want an adventure?"

The word "adventure" changed everything. As it turned out, not one of them had ever been to Indianapolis. A cabbie named Frank said he would drive me if I gave him the $27 right then and signed an IOU for $350 in front of everyone.

Fine. Off we went. But Frank wouldn't stop for anything to drink or to find a restroom. He drove relentlessly. When we could finally see the skyline up ahead, he started to shake. I thought we might never make the last three miles.

Meanwhile, Melvin had bought the Gimbels' building in New York and returned to Indianapolis. JoAnne told me later that she'd heard Melvin's voice on my intercom, so she asked him what he wanted. He wanted to see me in his office because I needed to go to New York right away.

> Come on! Do something different for once. You'll be able to tell this story for years!

JoAnne reported that I hadn't shown up for work that morning and hadn't answered my home phone. Melvin told her to call Aviation and Security and have them track me down. It must have been about two in the afternoon when our aviation department found out my plane had landed in Evansville around nine. At that point, they realized I'd been missing for five hours.

When the Evansville cab pulled up in front of our offices, all the valet guys started laughing and clapping. "Miss Eliz! Miss Eliz! Everyone has been looking for you," one of them said.

I crawled upstairs, dehydrated and hungry, and went to Herb's office where Melvin and all the development men were meeting.

"Where the hell have you been?" Melvin shouted.

"I need at least three hundred and fifty dollars," I said.

"For what?"

"I have a cab waiting downstairs."

Melvin never carried money, so he said to Herb, "Whatever her story is, I'm sure it's worth at least five hundred."

After I had entertained the guys with my story, they began razzing me about spending so much money on a cab. Melvin finally held up his hand and said, "Not one of you would have made it back here on your own. You would still be sitting in Evansville, waiting for someone to come rescue you."

For months afterwards, whenever I crossed paths with Melvin, he said, "Eliz, where are you going now?"

It didn't matter if I said LA, Phoenix or Atlanta, Melvin always replied, "Are you taking a plane, or should we just call you a cab?"

Then he shook his head and laughed all the way down the hall.

40

ON THE ESCALATOR
IN THE HYATT

"Hey, kid, where are you going?" Melvin yelled up from the bottom of the escalator.

"New York!" I shouted down from the top.

"Feel free to spend my fortune if you get into trouble out there," he said as we passed each other.

"Thank you, sir!"

41

MARKLAND MALL, MARCH 16, 1986

The Chicago Bears had won the Super Bowl. An unbelievable team filled with goofballs and characters, they swaggered their way into NFL history.

William Perry, aka the Fridge, became a star and media darling during the 1985 and 1986 seasons. Fridge T-shirts, Fridge hats, the Fridge dance. He was 320 pounds of fat and muscle, wearing a huge smile with as many gaps as teeth.

Because Markland Mall in Kokomo, Indiana, was close to Chicago, we decided to ask a Bear to the reopening of the mall. Shari Simon called his agent, and the Fridge agreed to appear. We were thrilled but also anxious because there were few things worse than advertising the appearance of a big celebrity and then having him back out. We also knew the Bears were so hot, public safety and security would be a major issue.

On Tuesday of that week, we got a call that the Fridge was taking his wife to the hospital to have their baby. He canceled. After a six-hour panic, we heard Jim McMahon was willing to replace the Fridge. A different kind of Superbowl shuffle! It was as though we were expecting the vice president of the United States, and he had to cancel but was sending his good buddy, the president.

Jim McMahon was a legend, a quirky quarterback who fought with and defied his coach, Mad Dog Mike Ditka. McMahon wore sunglasses indoors and out, and during games, a headband to keep his blond hair out of his aqua blue eyes. He was Chicago's sexiest guy, appearing on TV every day in some antic, commercial, or wise guy sound bite. All of a sudden, I didn't have any trouble getting people to work on Saturday. Every woman in my department wanted to go to Kokomo to glimpse Jim McMahon in the flesh.

About forty thousand people filled the mall and lined up. McMahon continued signing autographs even after his fingers started bleeding. I saw him change bandaids at least three times. According to his agent, Steve Zucker, McMahon only accepted about two percent of his offers for appearances, and his fees were high to discourage inquiries. Word had it that he had received $20,000 for an hour of his time the night before.

In our case, Jim wanted to honor the request from his teammate. Vic Ruthig told the newspaper that McMahon was appearing "out of the goodness of his heart and a generous donation."

Late in the day as the crowds were winding down, a few of us returned to the mall office and there—before our very eyes—was Jim McMahon's black leather coat, his scarf and sunglasses! I had his coat on my back before anyone could blink. The leather was soft as silk, the scarf cashmere, and everything smelled of his cologne. I closed my eyes and breathed in deeply.

Markland Mall was the lead story in the media for the next three days, but women in my office talked about that weekend for months.

42

DREAMING SMALL

While waiting for a meeting, I rummaged through the big black binders containing sales proposals, on Melvin's sofa. One of them caught my eye—a pitch from Genesco to sell Bonwit Teller, an elegant queen of a store on Fifth Avenue in New York.

The idea of this classic Art Deco building was so exciting, I started visualizing a new kind of vertical mall in the old, highly decorative space. A mall of imports, a mall of boutiques filled with the world's most exclusive and expensive merchandise, French lingerie, German eyewear, a vodka bar in the old fur salon!

Meanwhile, a man with much bigger dreams than mine was thinking about the ground lease and air rights to that spot, so he could build Trump Tower.

43

ON THE PHONE

I had just landed in Chicago and was preparing for what was to be a contentious merchants' meeting at North Riverside Park Mall. The phone rang and Melvin's secretary said he wanted to speak to me, so she was going to patch him through.

"Eliz, I want you to get on a plane and meet me here in Detroit," Melvin said loudly.

"Okay, fine. Why?" I asked.

"I am going to buy the Renaissance Center," he replied.

"Oh, no! I am not coming for that."

"Eliz, get on a plane!"

"No, Melvin. I'm here to take care of a real mall with problems that can be fixed!"

"Get here now!"

"Melvin, listen to me. Neither you nor I can save that ill-conceived piece of crap!"

I'm not sure who hung up first, but the Renaissance Center was never mentioned again.

Don't assume for a second that Melvin solicited my opinion often. Only three times in my years at Simon did he ask me what I thought—Detroit, the Gimbels' building, and Las Vegas. He knew marketing would be the key to success at each of those properties.

44

THE BEAT OF MY HEART

No matter where I traveled, no matter how many times I watched the brothers break ground to start a new project, no matter how many ribbons we cut to let throngs of shoppers into our latest center, my heart was in downtown Indianapolis.

We had zigzagged our way across America, changing the way people shopped and lived. We'd improved other cities, given their residents new retail choices, revitalized downtowns, and then flown home to our own urban core, in decay since the seventies when so many people had moved to the suburbs.

I wasn't alone with my dream. Restlessness invaded the Simon organization and people in all departments—development, leasing, architecture and construction. We longed to develop our downtown. We wanted to practice our skills at home. We aspired to build a mall we didn't leave behind, one we could bring our families to see and show them our work. A mall we could walk through, shop in, drive by and say, "That's what I do for a living. That's why I travel so much. I help make malls like this one all over the country."

In 1979, Simon & Associates announced its plan to build a downtown mall near the historic Monument Circle. They called it Circle Centre Mall. In 1985, a model of the mall was unveiled to the public, and the words "Circle Centre" became my dream, my goal, my blind spot, my weakness, and the beat of my heart.

45

THE INDIANA ROOF BALLROOM

Back in 1926, Edgar Hunter and Preston Rubush envisioned a ballroom designed to look like the plaza of a Spanish village. The ballroom was to be built on the top floor of a Spanish Baroque style building, the Indiana Theatre, in downtown Indianapolis. It would be called the Indiana Roof Ballroom.

Balconies with carvings and wrought iron overlooked the dance floor, and painted grapevines climbed the plaster columns and stucco walls. The huge room was a romantic fantasy with "the most comfortable dancing surface in the world," according to Lawrence Welk. The dance surface had two subfloors and a layer of cushion. The ballroom's most stunning feature was a midnight blue dome with tiny pale lights and a crescent moon that cast the whole room as a starry night. Patrons really could believe they were dancing outdoors.

For years, famous people and big bands came to the Roof—Tommy Dorsey, Louie Armstrong, Frank Sinatra, Bennie Goodman, Guy Lombardo, Doris Day, Cab Calloway, Bing Crosby. After the big

> I still have a bond with that building unlike any other, anywhere.

band era of the forties and fifties, the generations that followed weren't interested in ballroom dancing, and the Roof closed in 1971.

In the mid-1980s, Simon decided to restore the Roof to its former glory as part of the revitalization of downtown Indianapolis. To maintain the integrity of the original ballroom, we had to work with historic preservation and restoration experts. We could update electrical and technical elements but weren't allowed make any changes, beyond restoring and repainting, to the original structure or color scheme. The day finally came when the restoration was almost complete, and the historic preservation experts were coming to do their final inspection.

Later in the day, Herb called me into his office to tell me the experts were upset. Our designer had tried to match the original colors, but once the paint dried on the stucco facades and ornate woodwork, the colors weren't right. Consequently, the experts would not sign the release allowing us to open, and our grand opening was nine days away!

We already had parties, proms and weddings booked for the coming year, starting with our grand opening weekend with three big events, not to mention Tony Bennett was coming. RSVPs were flooding in, audio/visual men were crawling all over the ballroom, a film was being edited for the opening, and seating charts lay everywhere.

Herb asked me to drop everything, calm down our construction department, and work with the preservation people to re-do the paint. I spent the next week in the ballroom, acting as interpreter, colorist and traffic cop. I still have a bond with that building unlike any other, anywhere.

The day of our first party for the media, we again tested the lighting and special effects, having decided to enhance the night sky with lightening, thunder and falling snow. Nothing happened. We got no lights, no sound, no snow, and the hot shots who installed the technology had left town. We called in everyone we knew with any relevant experience to fix it.

The Roof opened to the public on a Sunday afternoon. Many people came to reminisce about the big band days and dancing with sweethearts and soldiers. More than one elderly lady told me that when she was a young woman, "The Roof actually opened up to the night sky." I heard so many stories of engagements, proms and weddings that it was no wonder to me the Roof had such a romantic vibe.

For those who believed they saw the Roof open to the night sky, felt the breeze on their bare shoulders, and cuddled closer to their honeys, I believe I saw it once, too.

46

IN MELVIN'S OFFICE,
JANUARY 28, 1986

Melvin's office seemed dimly lit, which I never understood because the room was full of windows.

Entering, one approached his desk from the side, not the front. I always had the impression I'd stepped into a strange, magical land where ordinary life was suspended and boundaries no longer existed. As if I were visiting the Wizard of Oz.

On that particular January day, Melvin sat in his usual spot behind his desk, his back to bookshelves with mementoes and a stunning photograph of his gorgeous wife, Bren. Three televisions in the wall cabinet to his left were each tuned to different news stations. The Space Shuttle Challenger was about to be launched after a three-day delay.

Our public relation's director, Billie Scott, and I were in the middle of a presentation as the countdown began. We all stopped to watch the launch, our eyes locked on the shuttle. Seventy-three seconds after blastoff, the rocket with seven astronauts inside exploded into a ball of fire. The image was shocking, unbelievable, unbearable, and tattooed on every brain that saw it.

I turned to look out the window, unable to make sense of the peaceful scene below in downtown Indianapolis. A moment later, Melvin picked up the phone, saying, "What's different?"

He then placed a call to someone who was clearly way behind him in processing what had just happened. Frustrated, Melvin hung up and started talking to Billie and me about things that would be different as a result of the shuttle disaster.

I can't recall anything he said. I was too stunned to think at all, and Melvin was already thinking ahead. Melvin's mind was always fluid, shifting gears without a grind. He made adjustments for changes no matter how they came about.

47

THE GREEN ROOM

After a trip to New York to research different marketing practices used to sell new office space and condos in the huge buildings bursting out of the ground there, I decided Simon needed a sales office in downtown Indianapolis.

Think in terms of a model home that builders construct to sell houses or condos.

I wanted to build a special space outside our regular offices that would be used only for marketing Circle Centre. It would be glamorous and full of renderings and architectural models that would convince storeowners to sign up for our downtown mall. I went to Herb to ask for permission to rent some space and build it out as a sales office. His answer was no.

After a few weeks, I prepared a presentation to show Herb what some other developers—none of them in the shopping center business—were constructing as sales offices. Again, his answer was no.

Perhaps I just hadn't found the right way to convince Herb that we really needed a sales office. The Simon corporate offices were in the Hyatt building downtown, so I started poking around there to see if anything was available. I got what seemed a sign from God when I discovered an empty space on the fourteenth floor. It was so perfect because the windows overlooked the dirt lots and huge demolition holes where our mall was to be built. I just knew Herb would change his mind! Remember, location, location, location. But his answer was still no.

Unbelievably, I made up my mind to rent the space anyway and went into collusion with Rodney Putz, convincing him to sign the lease. Then we built an exquisite space with walls painted hunter green. The Circle Centre leasing office was a gem of color and design with video screens, seating, a kitchen, and dining room. After a sales pitch, heavy drapes would electronically sweep aside and reveal the mall area fourteen stories below!

No one knew the room was taking shape, and even after it was finished, Rodney and I said nothing.

As we were preparing for a visit from Philip Miller, chairman of Marshall Field's, Herb admitted to me that he wished we had built a sales room. My moment had come! I asked him to take a walk with me, and we headed for the fourteenth floor. On the way, we gathered up Rodney and a few other vice presidents. When we entered the Green Room, they were flabbergasted.

As I explained to Herb the different marketing features and the way the room functioned, I could see him getting more and more upset. Maybe he was realizing how many of his employees had been tapped to help create the space.

He was shaking a little as he spoke in a voice I didn't recognize. "Get out of my sight."

In any other corporation, I would have been fired on the spot.

I ran to the safety of my office and heard nothing from him the rest of the day. But early the next morning as we gathered to meet with Mr. Miller, Herb patted me on the back.

The Green Room served us well. On one occasion it was part of a covert strategy to get the Simons and all the vice presidents to attend a special presentation. I went into work at seven one morning, sneaked into all the private bathrooms, and wrote on the mirrors in lipstick, "Meet me in the Green Room at four o'clock!"

Every single man showed up.

48

MONDAY NIGHT FOOTBALL

When the first Indianapolis Colts game televised from the Hoosier Dome was scheduled, our marketing department was asked to participate. Simon marketing would make sure the city had an unforgettable opening stunt for the game.

As it turned out, the game was to be played on Halloween. Vic Ruthig, Jim Austin, Kevin O'Keefe and Mark Craft came up with a great idea. When the show opened, everyone in the Hoosier Dome would be wearing a mask of one of the three game announcers: Frank Gifford, Al Michaels or Dan Diedorf.

The camera shots of the game audience in the Hoosier Dome were phenomenal! Indianapolis became the talk of football fans across the country. As it turned out, even the Nordstrom family was impressed, and would remark on our stunt in a meeting a few days later.

49

THE GREAT NORDSTROM CAPER

In yet another meeting about downtown Indianapolis, Herb said that getting a Nordstrom store in Circle Centre was our last hope. All the other flagship possibilities had said no.

The downtown mall was a slow, fitful work in progress, and we needed a store that was bold enough and imaginative enough to have confidence in our vision. Herb invited the Nordstrom brothers to Indianapolis, saying we would pick them up in Seattle and fly them to Indianapolis for the day.

In preparation for our meeting, I walked the route we would take on our city tour and visited the restaurant where we would dine with the Nordstroms that evening. The city wasn't looking good. Early November skies were low and gray, and chilly winds whipped trash and newspapers around the streets. Almost no pedestrian traffic was in sight since few workers even went out for lunch.

Acting on my own again, I decided to stage the downtown like realtors stage homes for sale. First, I called local modeling agencies and hired dozens of good-looking, well-dressed people to carry shopping bags and stroll along the tour route for three hours. Next, I was concerned that our wonderful restaurant, Peter's, wouldn't be full on a week night, but I felt confident the very handsome Gerry Kosene from Kosene and Kosene Development could fill a large dinner table with fabulous fashion people. Gerry agreed and I told him to send me the bill. Simon employees would fill the other tables. I also sent a message around that everyone should come to work dressed up the day of the Nordstrom visit.

By the time Herb, Barry Lindsey, and I took off for Seattle to pick up the Nordstroms, I had done everything I could think of to spiff up and accessorize Indianapolis. When we returned from the west coast, the first thing the Nordstroms saw as they walked down the jet stairs was the backends of a line of black limos. Each license plate was framed with "I'd rather be shopping at Nordstrom."

Two amazing things happened that day. I overheard one of the Nordstroms say, "The downtown isn't much, but anyone who can pull off a stunt like they did for Monday Night Football will market the hell out of the place." And the image I will never forget is Herb Simon on his knees, begging the Nordstroms to come to Indianapolis.

50
RIDING A MOUSSE

The Indiana Roof Ballroom was overcrowded with Simon family and friends gathered for a huge wedding. I had purchased a gorgeous dress for the event. The top was plain black to the hip where it exploded into a bright red satin skirt with layers and layers of tulle underneath.

Shortly after a sumptuous dinner, the wait staff started bringing extravagant desserts from the kitchen to an elegant buffet table of sweets. Cakes, pies, cookies, tarts, crèmes, ice cream—anything made of sugar was beautifully presented. A waitress carrying a tray with an enormous silver bowl on her shoulder walked out of the kitchen and began to cross the room. As she passed my table, a large man behind me stood up at the same moment I rose to go to the ladies' room. He knocked into me, and I bumped into the waitress, causing the bowl and its contents to crash to the floor with a loud clatter. The gigantic silver bowl full of chocolate mousse bounced and rolled across the dance floor, spewing soft, fluffy mocha-colored mousse in its path.

My heel slipped on the mousse, both feet went out from under me, and I slid across the dance floor, riding that mousse all the way! Horrified, I got up as quickly as I could and stood alone in the middle of the dance floor. The great mousse drop calamity had happened during a band break, so everyone heard the bowl hit the floor and watched me glide by. I looked down at my dress. I wasn't covered in mousse, I wasn't hurt, and everything appeared fine.

> My heel slipped on the mousse, both feet went out from under me, and I slid across the dance floor, riding that mousse all the way!

Then…globs of mousse started dropping from under my dress. Plop…plop…plop. Even worse, as the mousse began to melt, rivulets of chocolate drizzled down my legs and into my shoes. Plop! Drizzle, drizzle, plop. I was frozen in place by the realization that I must appear to be pooping chocolate. My tulle petticoats had swept up the mousse, and my body heat was melting it.

The wedding crowd seemed mesmerized. How bad would it get? Waitresses came running from all directions with towels to clean the dance floor, wipe my legs, and lift my skirt to shake off the mousse.

As it turns out, you can't really die of embarrassment.

Out of the corner of my eye, I saw Melvin approaching. He asked the waitress to bring me a blanket.

"Eliz," he said, "the next time you need this much attention, just set yourself on fire."

51

CALIFORNIA DREAMING

It was a neighborhood of empty lots and gated storefronts, continuous street traffic, drug dealers and users, prostitutes of all ages, their customers, transvestites, leather boys, and drunks passed out in hallways.

In this same neighborhood, tourists climbed out of buses, carrying cameras and wallets, ready to experience the magic of Hollywood. Their faces quickly registered shock and dismay. Where was the excitement and glamour?

Melvin Simon & Associates had purchased several blocks of Hollywood Boulevard along the Walk of Fame, one of LA's big tourist attractions. Simon was part of a major Hollywood redevelopment project that would include a three-level shopping center, two office towers, a four-hundred-room hotel, four restaurants, two hundred parking spaces, and a motion picture museum.

I couldn't wait to get my hands on this project. With stars in my eyes, I put together a California marketing team and headed for the left coast. A Holiday Inn was on the property, so Deb Coons, Jim Austin, Kevin O'Keefe, and I planned to stay right there while we set up the groundbreaking ceremonies, talked with new vendors, and got to know local politicians. We only realized how much the neighborhood had deteriorated when we were told that a police escort in and out of the hotel would be necessary. The hotel would also lock us in at night because of the crime rate.

The Hollywood redevelopment project won unanimous approval by the Los Angeles City Council planning committee. Following the announcement in the Los Angeles Times, a small group of homeowners in the neighborhood voiced objections, and a lawsuit was filed the following spring by one local resident and a group of outside activists. The suit complained that the size of our project would "raise the area's noise levels, ruin views, and create traffic gridlock that could stretch for blocks around the development."

I was astonished by the idea that anyone would fight improvements to a dangerous, seedy neighborhood. Development could transform what was a disgrace into a strong tax base for the community to continue its redevelopment and restore luster to the Walk of Fame.

The idea of building a motion picture museum was gradually gaining support in the film industry. A board of directors and a board of trustees were developed and a fundraising gala planned for April 1, 1989, in association with *The New York Times*. Stephen Spielberg was to be honored that evening at the Century Plaza Hotel in Los Angeles.

The board of directors was led by Sydney Pollock and included Barry Diller, David Geffen and Dianne Feinman. The board of trustees included Candice Bergen, Frances Coppola, Jane Fonda, Goldie Hawn, David Hockney, Mike Nichols and Martin Scorsese. Benefit committee members were Dan Aykroyd, Marvin Davis, Rhea Perlman, Danny DeVito, Richard Dreyfuss, Harrison Ford, Whoopi Goldberg, Jeffrey Katzenburg, Kathleen Kennedy, Norman Lear, George Lucas, Penny Marshall, Bette Middler, Martin Short, Steven Sills, Lew Wasserman, Jerry Weintraub, Robin Williams and Walter Zifkin.

Called the American Cinematheque, the museum was described as "a nonprofit, viewer supported arts complex of state of the art theaters, galleries and gathering places dedicated to the celebration of the moving picture in all its forms." The Cinematheque would show the best of film and video from the classics to the avant-garde, as well as programs from archival collections. City Councilman Michael Woo called it, "the Smithsonian of the entertainment industry."

The night of the gala, movie stars were everywhere. It was fascinating to see people I didn't know at all, but who felt so familiar. Not a bad crowd to have supporting the project. I figured in view of all this high-powered and political support, the lawsuit would dissolve. I forgot we were in California. Our attorney, George Mihlstin, said the project wasn't likely to be torpedoed by the lawsuit, but the groundbreaking might be delayed for six months. Simon had already agreed to significant concessions on the project, which included paying nearly $5 million for a computerized traffic system and other transit improvements in Hollywood.

We crept slowly forward on the project. Jon Jerde, famous as chief designer of the 1984 Summer Olympics, was chosen as architect of the retail component and the Cinematheque. He said, "What's being done in Hollywood now is a major step in reclaiming something that used to be, the wonderful mixed use, social, entertainment, retail activity center of Los Angeles."

We had the dream in place and the talent, money, and influence to bring it to life. Then a second action was filed against us. Simon had won the first lawsuit, so the group called Save Hollywood Our Town (SHOT) took its case to the California Court of Appeal.

There was something else, too, something more personal that touched our project. AIDS was epidemic in Hollywood, and three men who were chosen to be museum director died and were replaced during the five years we worked on the project.

Meanwhile, the groundbreaking ceremony was about to happen.

The night was beautiful, the food spectacular, and a small band played theme songs from the movies for a hundred invited guests and media. For safety reasons, we had gathered on the roof of the hotel parking garage. An impressive group of stars, politicians and dignitaries arrived. Debbie Reynolds, a big collector of Hollywood memorabilia, brought Dorothy's ruby slippers from *The Wizard of Oz*.

It was my birthday, and I felt reflective as I stood away from the crowd. My birthdays hadn't been celebrated when I was a child, but I knew my coworkers, many of them like family, had arranged a birthday dinner for me later. And here we were, producing an event that would bring significant change to Los Angeles and tourism in California. I felt grateful, challenged and fulfilled. What I knew how to do best in life was work, and I was in a place at Simon where my work was appreciated, my opinions valued, and my staff and I were trusted. In the middle of my mental celebration, a group of policemen approached me.

"I'm sorry, ma'am, but we have to ask you to close this party down," an officer said.

"Why? What's wrong?" We had a file full of permits to hold the party so what was the problem?

The policeman said, "You're over the limit of the noise ordinance."

"Oh, okay," I said. "We'll shut down the band."

"That's not enough," the officer said.

"I don't understand. How are these things decided?"

"Come over here."

The authorities had set up a gadget resembling a Weight Watchers scale, only bigger, that measured decibels. The meter had been placed on the garage wall, and its little red needle was jumping around. On the streets below us, drug dealers and prostitutes, some of them children, were hanging around.

"Officer," I said, "it seems to me that we have bigger problems here than being a few decibels over a line."

He agreed with me but said they'd had a citizen's complaint, and we had to close down. I couldn't believe it. We explained the situation to Melvin who thanked everyone for coming. Our guests started leaving, and the event whimpered to a close.

Despite concession after concession on our part, the lawsuits and harassment continued. In 1991, five years after it all began, we gave up the dream of "being ready for our closeup."

52

"This award represents the hope and the possibilities that exist in America for each and every one of us, regardless of our cultural background, our sex, our age, or the color of our skin.

My guidelines are:

- Be people oriented. At Melvin Simon & Associates we have many people who are on their way up; they need understanding and compassion.

- The word "no" often means "maybe."

- The harder you work, the luckier you get.

- Protect your integrity because your word is your bond.

- Have a dream.

- Stress education and biblical values."

Taken from notes Melvin wrote to prepare for his acceptance of the Horatio Alger Award.

53

FASHION ADVICE

Melvin and other industry leaders had been invited to a think tank meeting in New York to discuss what they thought the biggest problem facing America would be in the next ten years.

Melvin wanted me to attend with him because he said, I had "interesting thoughts about things."

I got there early, wearing my best suit with shoulder pads bigger than my head and took a seat by the elevator to wait for Melvin to arrive.

"Let's go, kid," Melvin said as he ran by.

I caught up with him at the room where a man was giving out information packets and name tags. "I'm sorry, Mr. Simon," the man said, "but we can't allow your secretary to attend."

"She's not my secretary, and I brought her because she has a very unusual brain," Melvin replied.

"I'm sorry, sir, only you are invited."

"But you don't understand, "Melvin whispered. "She has no filters, no censors in her brain."

"Again, I am sorry, sir."

Melvin turned and said, "Sorry, Eliz. Wait here."

I took a seat and spent the day reading. Melvin reappeared after about five hours.

"Well, what did they decide?" I asked.

"They think the big problem is going to be race relations, but I disagreed."

"And what do you think?"

"I told them it was women in the workplace!" he said, laughing. "See you later, kid." He got in the elevator and left.

I went to the airport to wait for a flight back to Indianapolis, thinking the day was lost except for Melvin's great punch line. But it turned out that day served me well. Melvin realized that wherever I was, if we were not in the home office, I would be looked upon as someone's secretary. He became diligent in setting me up as one of his trusted advisors in meetings with new associates. He also worked wonders for me in Las Vegas when we started to work on the Forum Shopping Center attached to Caesar's Palace.

I had been sent to Las Vegas two days ahead of Melvin for a big meeting about this new kind of mall development. The executives at Caesar's were reluctant to give me information I requested and avoided meeting with me. On the day of Melvin's arrival, I was supposed to go pick him up at the airport and brief him on my observations. The hotel representatives left for the airport without me, so it wasn't until later at the meeting that Melvin and I were in the same room together. The Caesar's people had been pulling out one idea after another.

"So Melvin, what do you want to do?" they asked.

He pushed back from the table and said, "How do I know what I want to do? You haven't given Eliz a chance to tell me what I want to do!"

Everyone laughed, but that moment changed my entire relationship with the people at Caesar's.

> "She's not my secretary, and I brought her because she has a very unusual brain," Melvin replied.

At the next Las Vegas real estate convention, Melvin pointed out a man in the developer's booth across the way. "See that guy?" he said.

How could you miss him, I thought. He looked like a prince with perfect posture, perfect tailoring, perfect hair, briefcase, shoes and watch. The kind of quiet tastefulness that said, *I have a fortune and I've had it for a long time.* A lot of guys in real estate were wealthy, but most of them looked like the money had appeared fifteen seconds ago, and they didn't know what to buy first. This distinguished looking man had caught my eye.

"What about him?" I asked.

"He looked like a hillbilly two years ago, a real bum."

He'd fooled me.

"But when he got money," Melvin went on, "he transformed himself. Made himself into a first-class gentleman. He even went to some ferkakta finishing school and took speaking lessons. I admire the poor son-of-a-bitch. I even thought about trying something like that, but I just can't control myself." He laughed. "Although I thought maybe something like that could help you…"

I felt a stab in my heart, and tears started to come. I always tried to look professional but evidently I was somehow disappointing.

"You see, Eliz," Melvin said, "men can show their position of wealth or power by their watches or their shoes. We know what to look at to judge each other. Women don't have that."

He paused and looked at me.

"You should buy the best briefcase you can and the best purses and then put them up on the table for a while at every meeting. That might help you look more like a vice president."

We had been standing side by side, looking across the convention aisle as he finished his fashion advice. He finally turned and looked down at my black and white suit, black shoes, and tasteful, small, gold earrings.

"Oh, hell, Eliz. What you really need is stilts and a dick."

54

MELVIN'S MANY VOICES

Most people have one voice. Not Melvin Simon. He had four.

There was the screaming, raging voice, full volume, letting you and everyone else know how dumb you were and just how badly you had screwed up. "Those mall signs are all wrong! What's wrong with you! They're not doing the job!"

Or he might scream, "Get in here, I'm going to rip your head off! Get in here, I'm going to rip your arms off!"

In the beginning, I thought the yelling voice was a part of his persona that he had no control over. Then one day, I realized he only yelled at me in the home office but never when outsiders were present. After that insight, I never cared what he said because I knew he was just blowing off steam. Once in a while I screamed back, just to egg him on until he ripped up papers or threw something. Anything for the cause.

Then there was the voice that was loud but high-pitched when he was impossibly tired.

"I can't keep a schedule like this! Are you trying to kill me?"

That voice came with any event that ran overtime. Overtime for Melvin started at eight p.m., and God help me if he was still stuck somewhere at nine. His exhausted voice touched my heart. I could fix mall signs or any other mistake, but I couldn't give him rest.

His teaching voice was mellow, deliberate and kind. When I heard that voice, I knew I could ask questions. I could probe. I had his attention until he felt I understood the opportunity, the problem or the risk. Those were the best times because I could never guess or anticipate what assignment I would be given next.

"Eliz, I was just in Las Vegas, and I love the Omni Max Theater. The guy who invented the process is somewhere in Canada. Go up and find him. Figure out how those big screens work. Can we bring it here? Should we have one in all the malls? Let me know."

And finally, the jubilant voice—full of melody and joy—was reserved for his family, mall openings, groundbreaking ceremonies, and his beloved Indiana basketball.

55

BLACK MONDAY, OCTOBER 19, 1987

The Dow Jones Industrial Average plunged 508 points, more than 20 percent of its value making Black Monday 1987 worse than the stock market crash of 1929, and the all-time worst decline since World War I.

Opinions were circulating in the media about the causes of the drop, along with dire predictions that the disaster was going to get worse.

"Financial institutions might be in trouble, small firms could be forced to close, large firms would have to cut back," experts were saying.

Toward afternoon, after having exhausted their brokers and money managers, all the Simon VPs gathered in Herb's office. The room was filled with gloom and anxiety. Melvin ran in, just back from somewhere. He seemed not to immediately understand why all the guys were so upset. After listening to their woe and pessimism, he sat quietly for a moment.

Then he turned and said to me, "Go to three secretaries on each floor and tell them that I don't own any stock, we have no money in stocks, and everything is fine here."

Happy to be the messenger for a man who wanted to put his employees' minds at ease, I set out on my mission. I felt gratitude and relief from every secretary to whom I passed his message. Melvin had realized everyone was frightened, needed reassurance, and he knew the fastest way to do it.

56

THE BEST
GROUNDBREAKING EVER

Jim Austin wanted to ask Doran Gazit to design an artistic stunt for our next groundbreaking ceremony. He was an Israeli artist famous for wrapping buildings and other large objects with brightly colored inflatable tubes.

"What if," Jim said, "when Melvin puts the shovel in the ground, inflatable palm trees spring out of the dirt?"

It was perfect for the groundbreaking of our exotic new mall site, Plantation, in Florida. But the stunt put our budget over the top, 25 percent higher than usual, so I went with Jim to Melvin's office for the presentation.

"Sixty thousand dollars! Are you crazy?" Melvin yelled. "I'm not spending that kind of money!"

"Melvin, we need to attract the media," I said. "Groundbreakings are happening every fifteen minutes in Florida! This is a new market, a much more upscale mall. We need something spectacular!" I paused. "Besides, your guest list is a lot longer than usual."

Melvin ripped our paperwork into small pieces and threw them at us. "Go ahead, spend my damn money! See if I care! It better work!"

We crawled around on the floor, picking up the pieces of our proposal as we headed for the door and Melvin kvetched, "Marketing will be the death of me! You people are crazy!"

That spring, we flew to Florida to set up the event. The day before the ceremony, everything was perfect. Doran had designed a wonderful group of inflatable trees for us. The stunt was surprising and visually terrific. The tent, decor, ceremonial shovels, and commemorative giveaways were all in place.

Early afternoon a storm blew in and knocked down the tent, scattering everything across an empty field. We scrambled to put the elements back together again for the next morning. At three a.m., the storm returned and stayed. We were wiped out and had to move the event indoors to our hotel. Obviously, an indoor groundbreaking was not ideal.

Still stormy the next morning, Melvin's plane was able to land. When we got word he was on his way to the hotel, Jim and I positioned ourselves by the front door. We were expecting the storm to look benign in comparison to what Melvin would do and say when he walked through the door. His limo pulled up outside, and we braced ourselves.

Melvin bounded out of the car, ran through the door, and grabbed Jim.

"Jim!" Melvin bellowed. "Did you see that game last night? This is the best day of my life!"

Melvin had Jim in a bear hug and was dancing him around the lobby. Indiana University had won the NCAA Championship the night before.

Thank God!

Melvin was devoted to Indiana basketball. Years earlier, when he was in the movie business and one of his films was up for an Oscar, instead of flying to Hollywood, he drove down to a basketball game at IU in Bloomington, Indiana.

We explained to Melvin all the problems with the groundbreaking, but nothing fazed him.

"Aw, that's all right. You kids always do the best you can. Don't worry about it," he said.

57

THERE'S NO BUSINESS LIKE SHOW BUSINESS

In a 1987 interview with *US Real Estate Week*, the reporter asked if Melvin had a choice, what activity outside real estate would he choose?

Melvin answered, "I enjoy the marketing and entertainment aspect of real estate, as I did making movies. I like to see things that are exciting. There's too much drabness in life. So I would say I would try to concentrate on the marketing and entertainment aspects of it."

"You're in show business," said the reporter.

"Development is show business," Melvin said. "Everybody's got their own little phrase for it. But that's what it is because what we're doing to get the public to come in and sample our wares, that's entertainment and that's marketing."

After that I told Melvin if he worked really hard and got lucky, he might end up with a job like mine.

Melvin and Herb were always open to big marketing ideas because they believed, as I did, that we always needed to be doing something new to connect with our customers in compelling ways. A shopping center would be successful as long as three key elements were present: an accessible location, a variety of stores, and varied price points of merchandise in those stores. At Simon we wanted to offer two additional things—a warm human experience and something special, better and new.

Marketing was changing rapidly in the eighties. For instance, rock and roll heard only on the radio could be seen on MTV. The introduction of the VCR fast-forward button sent the advertising industry running scared. Thirty-second commercials were compelled to catch and hold the TV audience just like programming. The brightest, brainiest, most beautiful and poignant commercials were born in the eighties. To survive, every entity, including shopping centers, needed to up its game. When Coca-Cola entered the apparel business and put its logo on clothing, Coke ads could be seen walking down school corridors and city streets. Clever marketing made Cabbage Patch Kids a national obsession.

To top off the advertising frenzy, McCann Erickson conducted some revealing research. They polled young children ages four to eight and asked them about ice cream, television, monsters and movies. Then the kids were asked, "Who is the most important man in the world?" Santa Claus came in third and Jesus Christ came in second. The most important man to those children was Ronald McDonald!

Marketing was being taken more seriously, and budgets began to loosen up for strong creative ideas. We were in a fight for discretionary dollars. Time and money were limited resources in everyone's life, and shopping centers had to compete with sports, movies, restaurants, night clubs, concerts, amusement parks and aerobic dance lessons. If our customers were at home, we had to pry them away from the TV, rental movies, cable services, treadmills, home computers and gourmet kitchens. The old days of shopping center marketing were over. The fashion shows and trip giveaways no longer generated the crowds our merchants needed.

About then, we discovered that one of the richest sources for blockbuster events and exhibits was our local museums. A relationship between Melvin Simon & Associates and the Children's Museum of Indianapolis resulted in two special events that brought out huge crowds.

Vic and I had gone to the Children's Museum to see an exhibit called the Secret Lives of Teddy Bears. We were captivated by the tableaux depicting what teddy bears did when humans weren't looking. The scenarios showed more than two hundred bears celebrating holidays like Valentine's Day, Hanukkah and Christmas; bears at the circus; bears at the beach, displaying lots of bear skin; and bears at Paddington Station. The only word to describe the exhibit was enchanting.

We contracted with the museum to redesign some elements of the display to make them easier to transport, and we found ways to enhance the interactive play in some of the settings. For instance, children could play with the Three Bears' house and dress bears in different costumes in the bears-at-play area. Sick bears were treated at bear hospitals where rips were repaired and stuffing replaced. We hoped book displays of classic bear stories would motivate parents to read to their kids. It was wonderful to be able to provide so much fun for children. I could hear them laughing and screaming throughout the mall. It was all music to me!

Mall tenants profited with unbearable sales.

Our next partnership with the Children's Museum brought us even bigger rewards. The museum was looking for a sponsor for a large touring exhibit of Jim Henson's new creative work starring his Muppets. The Muppets were the hottest thing on TV, and Vic and I decided we would sponsor the show if we could persuade Henson to do smaller exhibits that could travel to our shopping centers.

Well, Jim Henson and his associates were dead set against the idea when we first proposed a partnership. They had never worked with people outside their own corporation before and were not about to relinquish creative control over a Muppet display. After many trips to their offices in New York and slide shows of other mall exhibits, we convinced them of our sincerity and commitment to our product and to theirs. The result was an event called Muppetapolis that filled Simon centers for ten-day visits.

> A fabulous idea was like magic to me, lightening in the brain that demanded attention.

Central to Muppetapolis was the Kermitage Collection—an array of artworks by the old masters reinterpreted Muppet style. It included Kermit, resplendent in satin and striking a classic pose as Green Boy, a spoof on Thomas Gainsborough's "The Blue Boy," and a mysterious Miss Piggy standing in for the "Mona Lisa." We scheduled reading hours throughout the day, a boomerang fish contest, and giveaways.

Picture the mall. At eye level as far as you can see are Muppet events and displays. A little higher, bright banners beckon everyone to the heart of the exhibit, and towering above it all floats a colorful hot air balloon, its gondola filled with Muppet characters looking down into the atrium crowded with shoppers.

Muppetapolis and the reactions it got among customers young and old provided my department with some of the most gratifying moments in our careers. Not only did we get to work with the great Jim Henson and his brilliant staff, but we got to witness the real joy of success by all measures. On the business side, our research and sales figures from both partnerships told us that we had attracted the right crowds, we had entertained them, and that as a result, they felt good about our shopping centers.

These events lined up perfectly for the malls of Melvin Simon & Associates, so it was easy to get agreement from the Simon brothers on these kinds of ideas. But sometimes one of my marketing people came up with an idea so big and unusual that it took a lot of work to get it sold. That didn't stop me because I loved trying to sell someone else's great idea. My staff told me that if one of them had an idea and could convince me it was extraordinary, I calmly marched with staff in tow to the project manager and sold it on the spot. They don't remember me ever failing to sell their ideas.

A fabulous idea was like magic to me, lightening in the brain that demanded attention. It seized me so that the thought of it...so strong, so clear, so right...became an obsession. And nothing but that idea would do, no compromise, no second best. Sometimes when I was presented with a problem or challenge, I saw the answer immediately. From start to finish the solutions occurred to me. This ability may have been my only gift, but it was all I ever needed.

If the idea was my own, that was an entirely different story. I lost my calm, my reason, and the process became torture. I went into a furious promotional dance, trying to explain the idea to my staff who would have to believe in it to help me produce it. Then we went to whomever was controlling the budget on that particular project, and God help that person because I was relentless. I could not relax. I had to have the budget and I had to have the approval. I don't know where I got that tenacity and single-mindedness, but I inspired it in my staff as well.

After we pulled off one more fantastic event, we crept back to the office with bandaids and blisters, headaches and hangovers to celebrate our amazing luck at having such fabulous opportunities in our work. Vic and I always went to find Melvin and Herb, shake their hands, and express our gratitude for their belief and support. Once they had given us the go ahead on any project, they never interfered, so I always had way more than enough rope to hang myself.

On occasion the brothers asked members of my staff to explain their loyalty to me. I wish Melvin and Herb had understood that I treated my staff the same way the Simons treated me.

58

A MILLION HERE,
A MILLION THERE

American Express wanted
Melvin to come to New York to
pick up a million dollar check.

The money was the proceeds of a deal Jim Austin had put
together, allowing American Express to distribute its credit card
information in the malls. Jim and I went to see if Melvin would
come to New York with us to accept the check.

After we explained the deal, Melvin was quiet for several seconds.
Then he said, "All right, I'll still fly for a million."

As it turned out, the check was delivered to our office, so Jim and
I took it to the brothers who started celebrating. Melvin said, "All
this money, and we didn't have to do anything! It's free money!"
They congratulated us and encouraged us to continue with these
types of endeavors.

This windfall came about because Jim had seen that Simon was
large enough to be a force in the marketplace. At that time, we had
seventy-two centers and 440 million shoppers spending $7 billion
a year. Jim had asked me if he could put together a deal to leverage

those assets. I told him to go ahead because I believed in his idea and because Melvin had looked me in the eye and said, "When you get an idea, never be afraid to make a mistake in my name. I will always cover you."

So Jim came back to me with an eight-page proposal that addressed American Express's marketing objectives. It was terrific. Jim cold-called American Express and got a meeting immediately. It was a new and exciting area of business for us that enabled Jim to start raising money to cover our grand opening expenses, especially in New Jersey and New York where the media costs were exorbitant.

We heard Monsanto had developed a new product, colored glass, that they wanted to showcase to retailers. We sold them the right to build our convention space in Las Vegas, using their new product, and saved Simon its construction expenses. The best outcome of all was Citibank when Jim brokered a deal between them and RCA. Citibank paid $6.4 million to have point-of-purchase stands in the malls to give away their credit card applications, and RCA gave us a million dollars in electronics to use as raffle prizes for anyone who filled out an application.

This was all back in the eighties when a million dollars was a lot of money, enough to get Melvin on a plane.

59

Developer Herb Glimcher
was reading a local newspaper
back in 1979 when he saw an
ad to sell vacant railroad land
along the Hudson River. Most
people would have thought
the land was worthless, but not
Mr. Glimcher.

The land was located directly across from lower Manhattan with
easy access to the Holland Tunnel. He bought 120 acres and then
called Melvin who saw the possibilities immediately and called
Sam LeFrak, well-known for his massive residential projects.

Simon research discovered that an estimated $200 million in
consumer spending was leaving Hudson County because the
500,000 residents had nowhere to shop.

Another 180 acres were purchased.

In addition to a mall, the partners envisioned nine thousand rental apartments and luxury condos, four million square feet of offices, two hotels, a strip center, and a marina with a thousand slips. In preparation, the partners put in $3.4 million for repairs to the aging infrastructure, including gas, sewer, water lines and roads.

On my first visit to the site, I saw nothing for miles around except railroad tracks, rubble and deserted buildings. A strong wind off the water buffeted the group listening to Melvin's dream. He was on fire, describing the future of this desolate land. His exuberance made it impossible for me to remain skeptical.

I began thinking about my own plan to bring this colossal endeavor to the marketplace. The enormity of the development was thrilling and would change so much land and the lives of so many people. Directly across the water from where we were gathered, the twin towers of the World Trade Center served as a beacon of its time and a symbol of American ingenuity and perseverance. The Statue of Liberty was only three miles downriver.

And there I stood, listening to a first-generation American whose father, at the age of fourteen, had walked across most of Europe to reach a boat that would take him to America. I pretended it was the wind making me cry.

60
MORE THAN A MALL

Whenever we reported progress on any project, Melvin always asked, "What are we doing for the community?"

We would say, "We're building them a fire station" or, "We're giving the town a library."

Then he would say, "Do more." All in the Jewish tradition of heal the world.

61

A SMALL FORTUNE

One of Melvin's favorite quotes was, "If you want to make a small fortune in real estate… start with a large one."

62
COMPLICATED

My inter-office buzzer went off. "Melvin would like to speak to you. Please come down," a voice said.

"I'll be right there."

In his office Melvin asked, "Eliz, why is everything so complicated around here?"

"I don't know, Melvin. Tell me what you mean."

"If I call the accounting people and ask for a couple of figures, all of a sudden, I get a big book filled with numbers and comparisons. I can't find what I need."

"What else?"

"If I stop someone in the hall and ask a question, no one ever gives me an answer! They say, we'll get back to you, Mr. Simon. Then here comes another book. I can't get any help around here!"

"Melvin, there's an old saying that goes, when the king requests a cup, a chalice is prepared."

"I hate it. Now, I want you to call accounting. Here's what I need to know…"

63

FATHER OF THE MALL

Las Vegas (AP) [May 1989]—The man who helped transform America's cornfields and pastures into the phenomenon known as the shopping mall says he is upbeat about the future of his industry and America's economy.

Melvin Simon, who started in the shopping center game 30 years ago by leasing launderettes and developing small centers anchored by discount stores, launches his most ambitious project this month with groundbreaking for the Mall of America. The Bloomington, Minn., mall will be America's largest—big enough to include its own enclosed theme park.

Simon's giant new 4.2 million-square-foot Mall of America was one of the star attractions at the International Council of Shopping Centers convention in Las Vegas last month. It shared billing with other major Simon properties, including a major project he will be developing in France and a look at the unique renovation of the old Gimbels building in New York City.

"I'm very upbeat about the economy," Simon said as he stood in front of his company's booth at the annual conclave for shopping center developers, builders and retailers. "Everything goes in cycles, but I feel excited about the future. You don't lease (a center) depending on today's economy, but on what the future holds. The glass is half filled."

How many shopping centers does Indianapolis-based Melvin Simon & Associates own or manage?

Simon turns to an employee standing at his side. He's either lost track or is testing the employee.

"We have 207 centers in 38 states," the employee responds.

Simon smiles.

64

A LITTLE RESPECT

Every year we attended the
International Council of
Shopping Centers convention
in Las Vegas.

This convention was held to facilitate meetings between
department stores, boutique store leasing agents, and
representatives/developers/owners of shopping centers. Almost
the entire Simon corporate office had some part in making sure
we were prepared for the convention.

My marketing staff and I spent weeks, working to produce
brochures, videos, and leasing pieces on all of our properties. Jeff
Cross and his decor department made sure our convention space
had new design elements, appeared fresh, and showcased our
newest shopping centers. Then Deb Coons, Jeff, and I headed out
to Las Vegas to receive the enormous shipments of supplies and
work with the union guys to set up our Simon space. It took three
days to build out the 12,000-square-foot space with two large
conference rooms and eight smaller offices.

The front of our booth was accessible to the convention floor from three sides, and our Simon sign stood so high, it was immediately visible from any entry. Our continuous buffet tables served breakfast, lunch and snacks. Casual arm chair seating and open tables made our space as inviting as possible.

Although Vegas temperatures could reach the high nineties in May, the convention center management refused to turn on the air conditioning until the night before the convention opened. Every year Deb, Jeff, and I spent three days in sweltering heat, preparing our space. One year we finally asked the union guys to turn off the blistering overhead light to make the temperature more bearable. The union guys wouldn't even consider it.

I called Rodney back at the hotel and asked him to come over. Rodney's size and height generally made things go in his favor, but those lights were not going to be turned off for anybody. Rodney went back and forth with the union guys, and then exasperated, he reached into his jacket as if going for a gun and shouted, "Turn these lights out, or I'll shoot them out!"

We never had to ask again.

At another convention, Melvin started a large meeting in the conference room at 9:30 in the morning, and three and a half hours later, I noticed he was slouched at the head of the table, looking depleted. I scribbled a note, asking if he wanted food service in the meeting. Once he had read the note, he realized he needed food.

Melvin seemed unaware that everything there existed for, and because of, him. All the effort, time and money it took to stage the convention didn't make any sense at all if our leaders weren't at the top of their game.

Years later at convention time, Melvin asked, "Eliz, why do you treat me the way you do?"

"I am not sure what you mean," I said.

"You always look out for me."

"Melvin, don't you know that if you have a good convention, we all have a good convention? You and Herb are the engine of all of this," I said, gesturing around. "I treat you the way I do because I'm grateful, and I respect you more than anyone I've ever known."

"Respect?"

"Yes."

"Well, Eliz, in that case, it's mutual."

65

TRUMP

The eighties brought computers, AIDS, artificial hearts, forensic DNA, liposuction and the Trumps.

I had just been in New York for two days and was walking back into my office in Indianapolis when I heard Melvin screeching for me over the intercom. I told him I would come right down.

When I got to his office, he bellowed, "What have you done now? What have you done!"

I couldn't think of any slip, blunder or oversight on my part, but I never knew what he was going to see that I had missed.

"I don't know, Melvin. What's wrong?"

"Here's what's wrong," he shouted, pushing a New York tabloid in front of my face. TRUMP DIVORCE was the enormous black headline.

I could see the peculiar route Melvin's mind had taken. He thought because I was in New York so often and had attended an event or two where Donald Trump had been that the Trumps' divorce had something to do with me. I was kind of flattered and started laughing.

"Melvin," I said, "there are some things in this world that go wrong without any help from me."

66

FULL CIRCLE

My life was flashing before my eyes, but I wasn't dying. I was opening another shopping center.

Lincolnwood Town Center was a regional mall outside Chicago with ninety-some stores and two lead tenants, Carson Pirie Scott and Madigan's.

The project had been particularly difficult from its beginning because zoning battles had gone on much longer than expected, so now the project team was ready to celebrate. We had gathered in the mall for a small breakfast before the ribbon cutting ceremony.

After eating, Mr. Madigan asked if I wanted to walk with him outside, around the mall. We had a little time before the ribbon cutting. As we walked, we reminisced about the old Madigan's at 4030 Madison Street and the significance that working there had on my life. He said he was proud of my success, then he asked why I had never married.

"Do you regret not having a family?" he asked. "My family is my life's greatest joy."

I was caught by surprise although his question had been very much on my mind. I said I hadn't been ready in the past for a lasting relationship, but the people at Simon had helped me grow emotionally. I had been surrounded by good, loving people for over ten years and had seen committed relationships all around me.

"It's never too late to find love," Mr. Madigan said, smiling.

"Speaking of late, what time is it?"

"Five to ten…"

"Holy crap! You have to cut the ribbon!"

We ran to the first mall door we saw, pushing our way through the crowd standing in line. Of course, the door was locked. We ran to the Madigan's door, but no one heard us banging and yelling.

"The loading dock!" I shouted.

We started running again, and then we started laughing. We laughed so hard, we couldn't run because you can't laugh and run at the same time. Finally, we got to the dock and ran up the ramp, through the back corridors, and out into the center court as Vic was handing out the ceremonial scissors. Herb had been waiting for Mr. Madigan to start the ceremony.

"What happened? Where have you been?" Herb whispered.

"Can't talk," I gasped.

I caught Mr. Madigan's eye and the laughter began again. He was happy to be opening a new store, and I felt joyous, knowing how different I was from the young woman he'd met years before.

Just as my physical scars had been removed, my emotional scars were healing. I had learned to trust and make close friends. In relationships with men, I had learned to pay attention to what a man does, not what he says, and to understand the importance of respect.

> I was a person who saw the possibilities and humor in life, who loved many people and was loved in return.

The most important lessons were personal. I had grown enough to see that I was intelligent, kind, and driven by hope and courage. I was a person who saw the possibilities and humor in life, who loved many people and was loved in return. And I was grateful to be blessed with a soul that sang and an imagination that soared. For the first time in my life, in my early fifties, I recognized my desire for commitment, stability, and a happy home life. And I was, by then, healthy enough to look for a man with those same goals. I found him, twice.

On January 1, 1997, I married Dr. William Meek. Our blissfully peaceful union continued until his death twelve years later.

On September 7, 2011, I married Stephen Taylor, my dreamboat from the escalator. Inside our wedding bands are the initials N.M.W. No Matter What.

Mazel Tov.

EPILOGUE

The last time I saw Melvin Simon was about three years ago. He had been dead for two.

I wasn't frightened to see or hear him. His voice was the same as always.

The first thing he said was he had been dead long enough to have a complete understanding of his life. He saw the good and bad that people had done to him, but it didn't matter because he had perfect peace.

"Eliz, it's like this…"

My room filled with fragrance and song and a feeling of bliss impossible to describe. Then, as if he had shut a door, those things were gone.

Melvin encouraged me to write this memoir to show what I had overcome in life. He had seen that my story, like his and his father's, was one of risk, courage and hope. He said he would help me, considering it tzedakah. As I've been writing the past twenty-two months, I've felt his immense love for his wife, family, employees and his work. And I believe he has guided me to tell his story as part of mine.

Sitting here after reliving so much of my life, I feel nervous about saying the truth of how this book came to be. I worry about skeptics, worry I will diminish the book and end up a poor man's Shirley MacLaine…

But I know what Melvin would tell me. "I've never hidden from the truth before." And I'm pretty sure he would say…

"If they don't like it, fuck 'em!"

MY STAFF

Jim Austin

Betsy Brackett

Jeff Cross

Deb Coons

Marsha Cale*

Mark Craft

Jeff Dutton

Ron Tierney

Greg Perry

Billie Scott

Victor Ruthig

Diana Dietsch

Brian Hadlock

Scott Johnson

JoAnne Hancock

Teri Moore

Lynn Wilson

Rob Banayote

Doug David

Wendall Lowe

Lisa Harper*

Garnet Smith

Kevin O'Keefe

Shari Simon

Cindy Simon

Jenny Simon

Max Simon*

Robin Miller

Sally Eckman

Randy Rohn*

Doug Hviston

Deb Polk

Mike Murphy

Carolyn Peavler

Lisa Sabol

Joyce Dreesen

Laura Gibbons

Bruce Burton

Janet Diken

Sherry Yorn

Kent Iunghuhn

Mace Hurt

Mark Searles

Patty Brennen

Patti Callen

Ray Ann Bayless

Jim Morrow

Claudia Andrick

Carolyn Stuhldreher

Bob Mitchell

Scott Johnson

Pam Storen

Barb Carter

Mark Stein

Carol Spratt

Beverly Becktell

Norm Meltzer

Felicia Hester

Marnie Marshall

Suzanne Lowenstein

Greg Perry

Matt Bowles

Connie Vernon

Denise Roy

Betty Alberty

Martha Cummings

Sandy Schneider

Roz Carter

Bill Sanders

Jackie Freid

Carrie Obenchain

Scott Givens

Tracey Rea

Amy Feldman

Mikel Hartman

Lauren Eckert

Ward Beckham

Howard Caulderon

Cathy Chuvalas

Jeff Dutton

Patty O'Friel

Bruce Burton

Laura Gibbons

Carolyn Peavler

Pat Noverosky

Carol Greenwald*

Jeff Lovell

Cynthia Prime

Diane Phelps

Phyllis Tobias

Debbie Delaney

Diane Browning

* Deceased

ACKNOWLEDGEMENTS

Special thanks and gratitude to Jerry Garvey, Jim Austin, Victor Ruthig, Deb Coons, Diana Deitsch, Teri Moore, Mark Craft and Jeff Cross. I couldn't have accomplished this without your enthusiasm and encouragement. Thanks for all the meetings, calls and lunches.

To my editor Candace Denning who helped turn a dream into reality.

To everyone who ever said, "You should write a book," especially Audrey Larhman.

To my friends who listened to the constant telling of the same stories.

To my husband who let me live in the past for twenty-two months while I wrote this book.

To Mike Rubin and Mark and Brandon Rodger for their help in all things Jewish.

To Tom Mueller, photographer extraordinaire.

To Jeffery Wallace of J Wallace Creative for his insight and limitless talent.

To Lynn Wilson and Sandi Marks for their precise proofreading.

ABOUT THE AUTHOR

After leaving the Simon organization, Eliz became president and CEO of the 500 Festival for the Indianapolis 500-mile Race held annually over Memorial Day weekend. After leaving that position, she turned her attention to volunteering for the many charities and not-for-profit organizations needing help with planning events and fundraising.

Eliz still lives in Indianapolis with her husband Stephen and his shoes.